New Living

FRANK WERNER *Translated from the German by Russell M. Stockman*

in Old Houses

HARRY N. ABRAMS, INC., PUBLISHERS, NEW YORK

Editor: Nora Beeson

Library of Congress Cataloging in Publication Data
Main entry under title:

New living in old houses.

1. Architecture, Domestic—Conservation and restora-
tion—Addresses, essays, lectures. 2. Dwellings—
Remodeling—Addresses, essays, lectures. I. Werner,
Frank.
NA7125.N47   728.3'028'8   81–3487
ISBN 0–8109–1366–6   AACR2

CONTENTS

INTRODUCTION

Throughout history people have continually altered the places they live in, improving them, enlarging them, or making them more compact. And always they have had to compromise with what they inherited from former owners, as evidenced by the frequent deliberate reuse of earlier architectural features or traces of former arrangements. There are residential palaces in Sicily, for example, that have undergone changes for centuries and are today composites of Moorish, Norman, Mannerist, and Baroque styles, but are nonetheless imposing for it. The record of such practice in the Middle Ages is clear; the medieval homeowner had no qualms at all about demolishing whole complexes of buildings from earlier periods and reassembling their components in new ways, or adding to or changing existing structures with bits and pieces plundered from destroyed or abandoned ones. In our own century architectural pioneers such as Frank Lloyd Wright, Adolf Loos, and Henry van de Velde were frequently engaged in the renovation of existing interiors or entire structures. The Viennese apartments redesigned by Adolf Loos are perhaps the best-known examples of their efforts. Today's generation of architects, confronted as it is with layer upon layer of inherited styles, is especially attuned to such work, revealing an increasing commitment to the restructuring of older buildings. Exemplary for their sensitive yet creative treatment of existing architecture are Michael Graves's Claghorn House of 1974 and Schulman House of 1976, or Charles Moore's own house in New Haven from 1967 and the Cold Spring Harbor Laboratories he completed in 1977. By contrast, Italian, or even more obviously Swiss-Italian, architects have advocated for a long time a more abstract and analytical manner of adapting historical structures.

Today, perhaps more than ever before, we have a need for authentic residential structures from the past, preserved in their original condition so that we may have as accurate a sense as possible of the housing concepts of earlier ages. By and large only the most significant examples in terms of architectural history suffice for this purpose, and naturally our treatment of these must be different from that of more common older dwellings to be met everywhere. Aside from the fact that it would be impractical to attempt to freeze a given historical style in the more ordinary structures, it would be philosophically wrong as well. A building exists primarily, after all, for those who use it, and it is their fundamental right to make any changes to it that satisfy their particular wishes and needs. People living in a building naturally leave their marks on it, and it is only thanks to these traces that a building truly becomes a part of history, whereas a house from an earlier period, perpetually preserved in its original condition, is in fact ahistorical.

Current practice might well be illustrated by numerous exemplary renovations of immense variety. Accordingly, it seemed appropriate to include in this survey projects representing various degrees of accommodation between old and new, in no way attempting to be prescriptive. We hoped to present a colorful kaleidoscope of prevailing architectural thought and practice, convinced that by juxtaposing well-publicized projects and lesser-known ones, alternating the work of unfamiliar names with that of highly prestigious firms, we could do greater justice to the topic than by providing a handbook slanted by our own preconceptions.

If one examines the range of projects included in detail, the outlines of three separate categories become apparent in spite of the extreme diversity of their design concepts, of local tradition, and of the limitations of respective materials.

By far the greater part of the book is taken up by renovations, additions, and installations undertaken in the interests of conservation in the broadest sense. These are not so much projects expressly commissioned to preserve historical monuments—though a few of these are necessarily included—but simply designs that strove to alter as little as possible the appearance of the given structure, its atmosphere, and the charm of its materials. Such a motive is clearly at work in these projects, whether it was a matter of restoring a vast Baroque manor or "merely" adding on to a building from the 1930's. Given the similarity of motive, one can only be astonished at the wealth of possible design solutions, both where an existing structure has been entirely and professionally remodeled or where all that was required was minor reorganization in adaptation to modern use. Even in the case of architectural facsimiles with exteriors reproduced in precise detail—generally only attempted when local building regulations demand them—interior spaces have been created that compare quite favorably with those of many a brand-new structure.

It is striking how in many of the examples from this category, as for example in the Swiss farmhouse renovated by Theodor Meyer in Muttenz, the traditional hierarchy between the front and back facades has been questioned and even partially reversed. Heretofore the front of the house has been the representational public side, while the back was given a more casual, everyday aspect. Correspondingly, the distribution of rooms inside has placed the living rooms on the front and utility rooms to the rear. Two things have conjoined to change this. The less visible rear facade offers in many cases the only chance for "modern" expansion, and also today's residents tend to find the calmer spaces near the back much more attractive than the front rooms exposed to public view and to the noise of the street. Accordingly, an addition toward the rear often becomes the most important part of a house, producing a delightful contrast between the two now equally important facades, but one generally hidden from the passerby who sees only the historical front.

A further tendency worth noting in these projects is the frequent prominence given to historical details in renovation. In the manor house René Stapels restored near Brussels, for example, original features have not only been exposed, but they have been set apart as virtually independent art works in that fixtures and furnishings have been kept away from the fabric of the structure wherever possible. Similarly, though on quite a different scale, the firm of Dissing | Weitling has managed to transform a modest worker's dwelling on Falster Island and a farmhouse in Drøsselbjerg into residences of exquisite simplicity by reducing them as much as possible to their original pure forms.

The situation is more complex in the case of additions patterned after an original structure so as to produce an homogenous whole. Christopher Bowerbank's expansion of a London house is a particularly straightforward example of this approach. In it the style of the addition is strictly subordinated to that of the existing building. The completed project displays such deliberate formal unity that one can scarcely distinguish the new from the old. Hugh Newell Jacobsen has gone one step further in his design for the expansion of a nineteenth-century frame house in Chevy Chase, Maryland. Instead of approaching the assignment in the usual manner, he chose to create additional space by first stripping the house of all its latter-day accretions, then setting down next to it a nearly identical copy of its main wing. Finally, the firm of MLTW/Turnbull Associates has demonstrated a third possibility. It transformed a modest 1930's house in Palo Alto, California, into a spacious configuration of rooms by placing a new module only a few yards wide in front of it, creating thereby a new facade. With its partially glassed roof and subtly placed openings joining new space with old, the addition fits in perfectly with the original house, giving it a new and dramatic spatial dimension.

A regard for surrounding architecture is particularly evident in those projects where it was necessary to assimilate new work into an historical urban context. The house restored and enlarged by Eric and Elda Hoechel in Sidi Bou Saïd, Tunisia, and the apartment in the harbor complex of Portovenere, Italy, renovated by Arturo Belloni, demonstrate how ample room for creative design exists even in dense urban settings where change is tightly controlled.

Recreating dilapidated or demolished structures constitutes a chapter unto itself. The supreme example here is Friedrich Wilhelm Kraemer's reconstruction of a patrician mansion in Cologne, exhibiting a most successful compromise between municipal preservation requirements and the needs of the building's occupant. Even relatively unprepossessing structures like sheds and warehouses can inspire exciting new spatial arrangements. Remarkable here in our examples—by Dissing + Weitling in Copenhagen, Jon Michael Schwarting in New York, and Juan C. Bertotto in Savannah, Georgia—is their refusal to reduce preindustrial or early industrial utilitarian structures to mere shells, more or less charming, with completely modern interiors, and their insistence on incorporating their characteristic details as indispensable components of the new design.

The architects represented by the second largest group of examples in this collection have approached historical buildings in a totally different way. For them old buildings are treated more like *objets trouvés* to which they can react with sympathy or violence as they choose. They do not simply accept a building's structure as binding, but rather attack it, reshape it, visibly altering the interior or exterior—or both. The historical use and context of the building naturally plays a subordinate role in the thinking of this group of designers.

An outstanding example of this more dialectical approach to architecture is the farmhouse near Urbino which was restored and enlarged by Piero Frassinelli. Especially provocative is the manner in which structures of a strictly purist, abstract idiom have been superimposed on an anonymous dwelling typical of its region. A rigid regard for symmetry has governed the placement of smooth, rectangular blocks against the gable ends and the one long side, just as it determined the arrangement of the four square rooms on the second story. A further jarring element is the glass roof over the block on the long side, extending as it does into the main roof and dividing it into two equal halves. Inside, the visual focus of the whole structure is the sunken square surrounded by columns and with a fireplace at its center that defines the ground-floor living room, a space extending outward to the exterior walls on either side. As it happens, however, this focal point is shifted somewhat away from the central axis of the house, a distortion precisely designed to lend a note of tension to the overall design. Here the inherited and the new have been forced into a union characterized by contrast, discord, and icy calculation, yet thanks to the severely abstract shapes of the additions, which in no way betray their residential function, the older structure is minimally compromised as an historical document. Perhaps the most remarkable thing about this house is the fact that though everything suggestive of bourgeois coziness has been banished, there is nonetheless an undeniably livable air about it. Its atmosphere is admittedly quite different from that of the charming house Charles Moore designed for himself in 1962 in Orinda, California, where once again a living area was marked off by columns. The comparison is appropriate if only because Charles Moore is also represented in this selection by a project—albeit a much later renovation—in Essex, Connecticut, undertaken by his firm of Moore, Grover, Harper. In contrast to the Italian example, the exterior in this case was hardly touched, so that it preserves an integrity virtually unrelated to that of the radically altered interior. The architects have dealt imaginatively with the oppressively small interior spaces by placing walls at angles, breaking through large openings between rooms, and stacking diagonal flights of stairs above one another. The result is a spacious, open configuration extending through all three floors, with innumerable cross views and calculated glimpses of height and depth that give it a somewhat theatrical air. The brilliance of the design only becomes evident when one recognizes how a conventional facade so primly belies the existence of this startlingly imaginative interior.

Quite a different approach, again, is revealed in the example of a carriage house converted by Crissman & Solomon in Andover, Massachusetts. Here the interior and exterior comprise a single homogeneous design-whole. The imposition of diagonal structures on conventional ones and the substitution of unmistakably modern windows for the originals have virtually obscured the former function of the structure. Historical forms have been paraphrased so subtly that only an expert could visualize today the original condition of the building, yet it is precisely thanks to this interplay that the house now seems so alive. The corner row house in Cologne, renovated by Planning Group BOS, represents a German counterpart to this approach. Here, both inside and out, the severely Expressionist brick structure has been enlivened by the addition of bold, contrasting forms.

The last and a unique example from this category is the apartment in Elkins Park, Pennsylvania, renovated by Robert A. M. Stern. The success of this project proves that even the most unpromising of modern one-floor apartments can be transformed into uncommonly complex spaces by the deft use of room dividers. Here the motivation was a desire to make a bland, predictable space more intriguing.

The third and final category is made up of projects having little to do with the renovation of older structures as such. Here we encounter alterations and extensions that could for all practical purposes exist on their own quite separate from the historical context into which they have been placed. In these cases the original architecture was merely the stimulus, a starting point; what is significant is the modern architectural response. To be sure, a certain unity between old and new has been achieved, but generally only on an abstract and intellectual level.

Perhaps the most important example from this category is Stanley Tigerman's conversion of a barn near Burlington, Wisconsin. "Conversion" in this case is a gross understatement. Even though portions of the original framing were used, the finished structure is essentially a new one in place of the old. Clearly it was a part of the design concept to reinterpret the conventional image of a barn in quite a free and ironic manner. Just as from the outside the irregular fieldstone masonry and the general outline of the structure are the only reminders of what a barn should be, inside there are only remote allusions to the building's original function. Most obvious of these is the attempt to preserve the feeling of great open space. The larger rooms flow into one another, grouped around a central core containing the kitchen, baths, and furnace room, thereby leaving the perimeter of the structure free of smaller partitions. Considerably more direct than Tigerman's work is Ari Bahat's treatment of a vacation house in Westhampton Beach, New York. Here the original structure was made into a pedestal for an added terrace and viewing dome. The result lays no claim to profundity, but it is a rather pleasant compromise between the "handmade house" style and professional architecture.

More self-conscious, again, are a number of additions that use an historical structure as a support, but which could otherwise stand as autonomous structures complete in themselves. A prime example is Jacob Blegvad's addition to a house in Hasseris, North Jutland. The parallel tubes of steel and glass above a swimming pool, conservatory, and fireplace and dining area stand out against the turn-of-the-century villa in such violent contrast that the viewer's whole attention is arrested by the resultant discord. Moreover, the appendix is absolutely self-contained in terms of function and design, sufficient unto itself, perfectly conceivable apart from the original building. On closer examination the addition to a London row house by Martin Crowley and Robin Moore-Ede proves to be a similarly independent design statement, consisting primarily of a single sheet of glass that only happens to lean against the rear facade of an older structure. The historical building acts solely as support for a framework that in fact has no further need for the structure it protects. A stimulating tension between old and new is the result.

Glancing once more in closing at the various projects brought together in this book, it becomes clear how the boundaries between my main categories begin to blur, how open the various design strategies are, and how much room for individual solutions remains. There are no prescriptions to be made toward a proper approach in the planning of architectural conversions; doubtless there never were. If yesterday's planners demanded a "future for our past," we are rather more inclined today to make the past work for the present. We are having to challenge history in fulfilling the tasks of our own time. Today there is perhaps greater danger that forward-looking thinking will be nipped in the bud than that our architectural past will be wantonly destroyed.

1. OLD AND NEW IN DRAMATIC CONTRAST

Conversion and Expansion of a Farmhouse near Urbino, Italy
Architect: Piero Frassinelli

One could scarcely imagine old and new in more severe juxtaposition than that provided in this example. The structures attached to three sides of the carefully restored old brick building are striking not only for their strictly cubic forms but also because of their covering of precisely placed white tiles, an exterior treatment totally at odds with the original structure. The glass roof above the middle extension is another element of deliberate estrangement. Under this roof a staircase connects the upper and lower floors, closing what appears to be a cut through the structure made by a giant routing machine.

In spite of these rather violent changes the original character of the old structure has been remarkably well preserved on the outside. Inside, however, new wall and ceiling panels in strong blues and greens, and smaller details in a severely modern idiom, break sharply with the impression of the exterior. The original beams and the outside walls are the only reminders of the house's former structure.

The severe symmetry achieved by the central placement of the glass roof on the outside is observed within only on the upper floor, where a central hallway runs between symmetrically placed bedrooms and baths. The living room occupies what was originally a stall on the ground floor, and it lies off center. It is dominated by four masonry columns at the corners of a sunken seating area encircling the fireplace. The kitchen is cut off from the living room by a diagonal wall—once again a startlingly modern feature.

Next to the living room is a complete bachelor apartment, which is totally separate from the main dwelling. The extensions on this side house a bedroom on the left, and on the right a storeroom and bake oven.

1. *Since the conversion the entry side of the house is doubtless the most dramatically impressive one. From without one cannot suspect the functions of the three new extensions. In fact, the one on the left encloses a courtyard, the central one houses the staircase, and the one on the right contains a small bedroom.*

1

2

2. *The back view is somewhat less shocking. The glass insert into the roof cuts across the whole house, providing light for the upper floor.*

3. *Of the two structures extending out from the bachelor apartment, the right-hand one contains a bake oven and a storeroom, the left-hand one the apartment's bedroom. In the background on the left the projecting framework of the staircase extension is visible, its glass panels continuing the line of the main roof.*

3

4. *The disorienting effect of the glass roof is even greater inside than out. Here the exposed beams above the central upstairs hallway are the sole reminders of the original structure.*

5. *Looking from the old structure into the new staircase extension. The rectangular framework of the glass roof is repeated in the glass screen that divides the stairwell from the main structure.*

6. *Floor plans (ground floor and second floor). Legend: 1 living rooms, 2 kitchens, 3 bedrooms, 4 baths, 5 storeroom, 6 courtyard.*

7. *View of the upstairs hallway. The connecting bridge is reached by means of a spiral stair and gives access to the dormer rooms on either side (see fig. 4).*

8. *The focus of the ground-floor living room is an imposing fireplace, recessed into the floor to form a seating area, and surrounded by four supporting columns.*

7

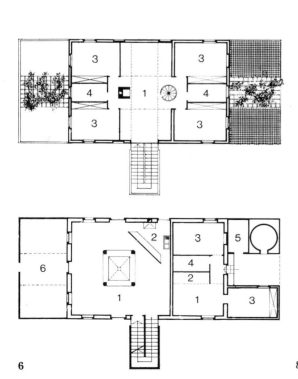

6

8

2. LIVING IN THE GRANARY

Restoration and Conversion of a Barn at Ittigen Farm, Canton Berne, Switzerland
Architect: Frank Geiser

This farm complex, dating from the fifteenth to the seventeenth centuries, enjoys landmark status and comprises five buildings in all: a farmhouse, the main dwelling, a great barn, a smaller barn, and the granary. Within the framework of the gradual restoration of the whole complex the architect was asked to salvage the dilapidated granary and adapt it to a new function.

In floor plan the elongated building shows the form of a rhomboid. Originally it housed a washhouse, bake oven, and partially open carriage shed on the ground floor, five separate storerooms for grain on the second floor, with a full-length attic above them. Toward the end of the seventeenth century an elegant two-room apartment was built on the ground floor, but, as a result of the installation of a workshop in the west end of the building around 1920, it had been to a great extent demolished. It has now been restored essentially to its original condition. A second apartment was created in the former baking shed, with side rooms appropriated from the aforementioned workshop. The five storerooms and the attic above them were converted into duplex studios, accessible from the balcony that runs along the courtyard side.

The building was so derelict that it first had to be dismantled down to the level of its solid sandstone foundation, each piece subjected to separate treatment and inspection. It was then rebuilt in its original form, using wherever possible original elements such as rafters, purlins, posts and beams, bricks, door and window fittings, grills, ovens, and tiles.

1. *Before the renovation of the granary the beauty of the half-timbered construction was visible only to the most discerning eye.*

2. *After reconstruction the elongated building presents itself again in all its original splendor. The granary was in such terrible condition that it was necessary to dismantle it completely down to the sandstone footings, subjecting each piece to a thorough inspection.*

3. *Site plan. Legend: 1 farmhouse, 2 granary, 3 great barn, 4 main dwelling, 5 small barn.*

1

2

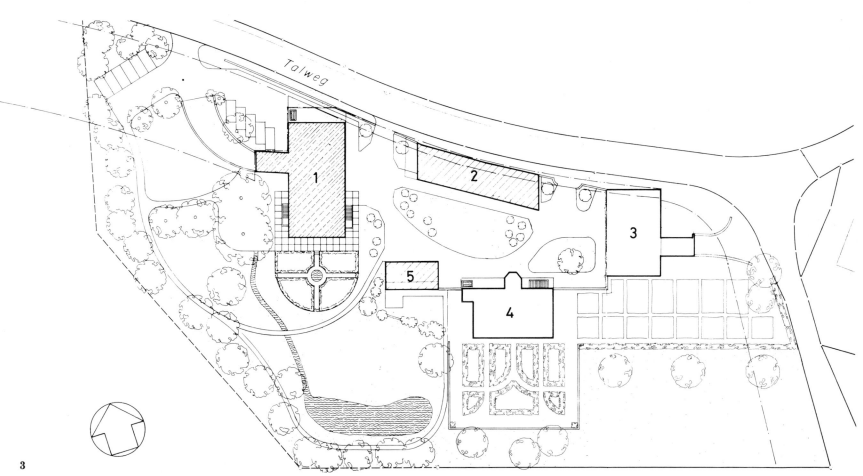

3

Talweg

1

2

3

5

4

4

4. On the courtyard side the wood siding contrasts strikingly with the whitewashed stone of the middle section, its ornamental shutters, and the round arches above the door and window openings. The upper story is dominated by the wide balcony that wraps around three sides of the structure.

5. The balcony provides access to five duplex studio apartments which utilize the former attic space.

6. Floor plans (ground floor, second floor, and attic) and cross section. Legend: 1 cellar, 2 laundry, 3 bedrooms, 4 baths, 5 kitchens, 6 dining areas, 7 living rooms, 8 balcony.

7. General view of the Ittigen farm courtyard. The granary, visible on the right, conforms fully to the residential character of the whole complex.

5

6

7

17

8. *The delicate mullions of the arched windows set the tone for the interiors of the middle section, here the living room of the original seventeenth-century apartment.*

9

9. *The studio apartments have sleeping lofts directly under the eaves, accessible by means of steep staircases leading up from the living rooms. The lofts are lighted by dormer windows that break through the line of the roof on the courtyard side.*

10. *Living room and kitchen area in one of the studio apartments. The character of these interiors is provided by the contrast between the whitewashed walls, the warm wall and floor tiles, and the variety of wood textures.*

10

3. STUDIO IN THE STALL, LIVING ROOM IN THE BARN

Conversion of a Farmhouse in Fulenbach, Canton Solothurn, Switzerland
Architect: Roman Lüscher

This building, dating from 1837, was not especially notable architecturally, but the owners nonetheless wished to preserve its character, altering the exterior as little as possible. Particularly they wished to leave untouched the massive roof and the quarry-stone walls of the living section.

The threefold division typical of farmhouses in this region, with threshing floor, stall, and wagon shed comprising an agricultural complex on one end, the dwelling proper in the middle, and a barn on the other end, proved quite appropriate to the new uses to which the building was to be adapted. The agricultural section, which was in poor condition and had to be completely renovated, came to house the client's living room and the studio in which he works as artist and engraver. The former dwelling section was able to accommodate the parents' and children's bedrooms, as well as three rooms for the client's father, who lives with them, with scarcely any change from the original floor plan. These two sections are connected by a balcony on the upper level.

In order to achieve a maximum of light in the living room and studio without violating the building's proportions by introducing larger glass surfaces, three-dimensional frames were set into the existing openings, with the glass alternately on the inside and outside.

1. *View of the house from the street, with yard and driveway. On the far left is the studio with rooms for printing and etching, in the center the dining room, and on the right the father's apartment. Above the latter are the children's rooms and the master bedroom.*

1

2

2. *On the garden side the structure rests directly on an expanse of lawn. Visible on the right is the beginning of the window wall of the living room shown in fig. 3 with its striking repetition of formal elements. In the center is a small terrace outside the kitchen. One staircase leads down into the cellar, and another up to the bedrooms on the second floor.*

3. *The living room lighted by this wall of windows stretches across the dining area to the street side of the house with its similarly treated windows.*

3

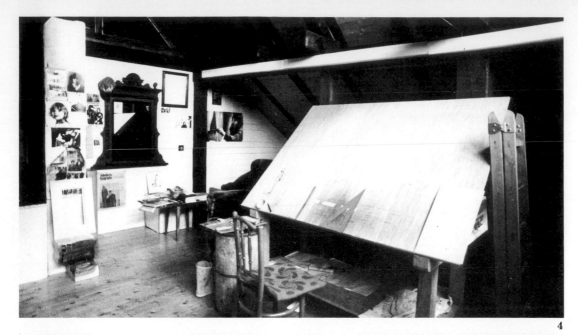

4, 5. The upper spaces of the studio are lighted by a row of gable windows. A steep staircase leads from the drafting area up to a gallery built right under the eaves.

6. Floor plan (ground floor) before renovation. Legend: 1 barn, 2 bedrooms, 3 storeroom, 4 dining area, 5 kitchen, 6 toilet, 7 threshing floor, 8 entryway, 9 stall, 10 feeding stalls, 11 wagon shed.

7. Axonometric floor plans (ground floor, second floor, and attic) after renovation. Legend: 1 barn, 2 father's apartment, 3 baths, 4 laundry and mud-room, 5 kitchen, 6 terrace, 7 dining area, 8 living room, 9 printing and etching area, 10 master bedroom, 11 children's rooms, 12 children's play area, 13 storage space, 14 drafting area, 15 play room, 16 balcony, 17 sitting room, 18 guest room, 19 studio gallery.

8–10. The living room is dominated on the one hand by the window wall, the sculptural lines of which relieve the regularity of the beams and rafters, and on the other hand by a massive fireplace. The unpretentious furnishings are appropriate to the farmhouse atmosphere.

4

5

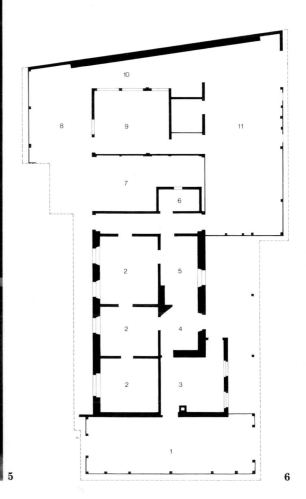

6

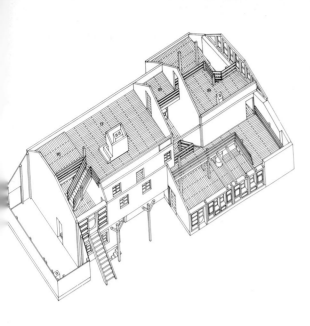

8

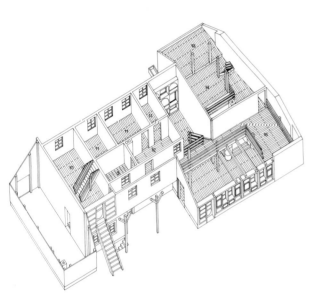

9

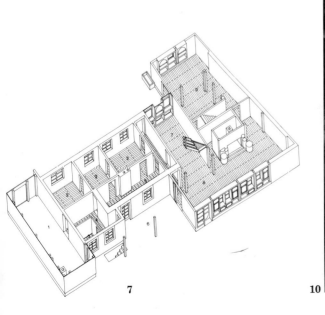

7

10

4. PRESERVING A LIVING TRADITION

Conversion of a Farmhouse in Muttenz, Canton Basel, Switzerland
Architect: Theodor Meyer

Muttenz is an ancient village along a single street, its farmhouses lining the road like pearls on a string. The buildings nearly touch each other at the sides; at most they are separated by narrow driveways. Occasionally they are set back a bit so that there is room for a small garden in front. A threefold functional division into stall, barn, and dwelling is characteristic of the structures, and these uses are reflected in the facades as well.

The owner wished to preserve this division, not only visually but functionally as well, and the original barn door was to remain the main entry into the house. The barn area itself became a spacious foyer, while the former stall and the toolshed behind it were transformed into an architect's office. A small one-bedroom apartment was created from the ground floor of the original dwelling, and the upper floor as well as the space above the former toolshed were converted into the architect's own living quarters. Access to this upper dwelling is by means of a spiral staircase built into the entryway.

Changes of floor level and differing ceiling heights were deliberately preserved so as to accent each separate space and set it apart. The generous dimensions of the structure as a whole, expressed for example in the imposing passageway into the barn, stand in delightful contrast to the small size of the individual rooms.

1. *Set well back from the right-of-way, the street facade clearly betrays the three-part division of function inside the house. The barn in the middle has been converted into a spacious entryway, the former stalls to the left now house offices, and the dwelling section on the right has now been expanded across the entire second story.*

1

2

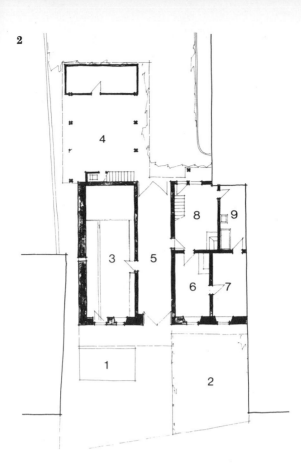

3. *Floor plans (ground floor and second floor) and cross section after conversion. Legend: 1 architect's office, 2 conference room, 3 furnace, 4 additional offices, 5 archives, 6 terrace, 7 entryway, 8 kitchens, 9 living rooms, 10 baths, 11 spare room, 12 master bedrooms, 13 dining area, 14 balcony, 15 children's rooms, 16 utility room, 17 guest room.*

3

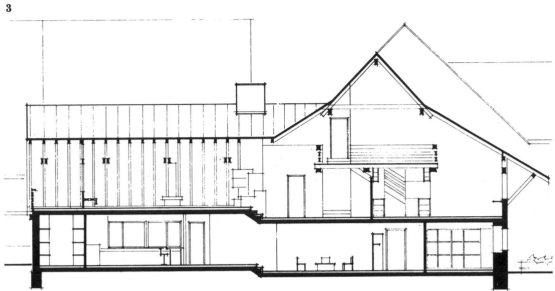

2. *Floor plan (ground floor) before conversion. Legend: 1 manure bin, 2 kitchen garden, 3 stall, 4 toolshed, 5 barn, 6 living room, 7 bedroom, 8 kitchen, 9 bath.*

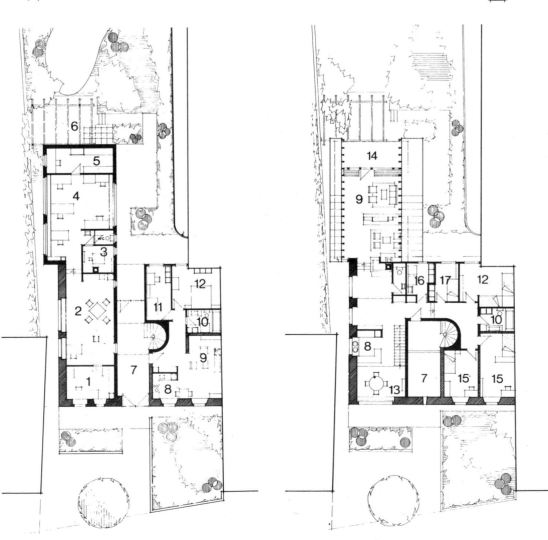

4

4. *The back yard is idyllic. Narrow as any city garden, the space had to be carefully apportioned.*

5. *View from the garden of the former shed wing which now houses offices on the ground floor and the living room of the larger dwelling above.*

5

26

6. *This view from the balcony above the entryway into the upstairs apartment reveals the clean carpentry characteristic of the renovation and so appropriate to the structure as a whole.*

7. *The living room of the main dwelling. In the background is the balcony mentioned in fig. 6.*

6

7

5. DIAMOND IN THE ROUGH

Modernization of a Landmark Farmhouse in Franconia, West Germany
Architect: Peter Reisser

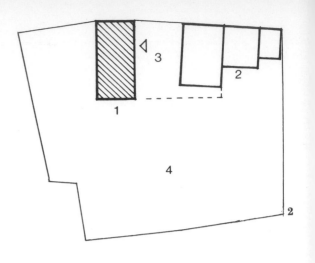

This farmhouse enjoying landmark status occupies a site of roughly 43,000 square feet and comprises, in addition to the main house and stalls built around 1870, various attached barns, the largest of which is roughly the size of the house itself. Between the first barn and the house lies the courtyard, closed in by a fence on the remaining two sides.

The threefold division of the elongated house was preserved in the remodeling: the kitchen and living quarters remain as they were; the bedrooms, separated from the former by a hall running the full length of the house, were converted into a large living room, utilizing an already existing storeroom, bath, and toilet. The stall, finally, with its lovely Bohemian vaulting, is today a spacious living room and gallery. The entire lower floor was paved with Solnhofen tiles.

In the front part of the second floor there were originally two bedrooms, as well as rooms for maids and hired hands. Guest rooms and the children's bedrooms were located here. The rear section now houses a large bed-sitting room, and the former grain-storage space above the front rooms has been converted into an open gallery reached by a winding stair from the sitting room below.

1

1. *The house directly abuts the street, and from outside it appears rather stark and formidable. The simple stucco and the window arrangement are typical of farm buildings in the region.*

2. *Site plan. Legend: 1 house, 2 barns, 3 courtyard, 4 garden.*

3. Floor plans (ground floor and second floor). Legend: 1 living room, 2 dining room, 3 kitchen, 4 toilets, 5 baths, 6 pantry, 7 living room and gallery, 8 fireplace, 9 guest room, 10 children's rooms, 11 bed-sitting room.

4. View of the house from the garden. The very large structure appears deceptively small.

5. Concrete slabs on the terraces clearly reveal the owner's choice not to aim for an artificial rusticity, as do the interior renovations.

4

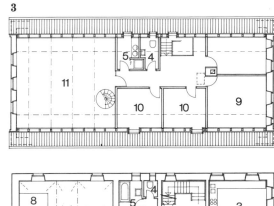

3

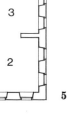

5

6. This living room functions as the center of the house. One enters it directly from the street. The Solnhofen floor tiles extend throughout the entire ground floor.

7. The dining room is reached from the living room and sits together with the adjacent kitchen on the street end of the house.

8. The staircase in the central living room. The natural wood paneling and the contrasting black stair facings attest to the owner's efforts to compromise between the traditional forms of the building and his own modern tastes.

6

7

8

9. *The bed-sitting room on the second floor extends upward to the eaves. It is available as a playroom for the children as well, whose own small rooms are on the same level.*

10. *Guest rooms under the eaves are characterized by the natural wood paneling of the sloping ceilings.*

9

11

10

11, 12. *The large living room and gallery has a vaulted ceiling resting on stone pillars. The paintings on the walls are the work of the owner of the house, one of Germany's foremost artists, and of various friends.*

12

6. FANTASY IN WHITE

Modernization of a Farmhouse in Fischerhude, Lower Saxony, West Germany
Architect: Horst Cyrus

This example of a 200-year-old farmhouse in Lower Saxony is a superb blend of modern elegance and traditional rusticity. The renovation work was by no means timid; all of the features that were kept have been altered by means of new materials, design details, and paints.

In order to mask all the irregularities and scars from its long history, the masonry of the nearly 40 × 75 foot structure was given a coat of white paint, pulling the whole together. Even the small-paned windows and doors, which had been selected after thorough study in the museum village of Kloppenburg, were painted white. A red tile roof was replaced by one of thatch, with a few new lights cut into it so as to illuminate recovered attic space.

The exterior and interior form a creative unity. The generous room dimensions typical of Lower Saxon farmhouses were generally preserved. Details such as the slender iron railings on staircases and balconies and the rectangular cut through the ceiling around the fireplace chimney were intended to heighten the sense of space. All such structural elements again were painted white.

The main ground-floor room is the 1,600-square-foot living room with the fireplace in the center. Next to it are the open kitchen, with eating space and utility rooms, a studio, and a spacious bathroom. On the east side of the second floor there is another living room connected to the one below by the opening around the chimney, and on the west side there are a guest room and two servants' rooms. High under the eaves on one end is the owner's sleeping loft, reached by means of a spiral staircase. A similar loft on the opposite end provides a sculpture balcony and space for meditation.

1. *The entire structure, including the small-paned windows and doors, was given a coat of white paint so as to mask the irregularities in the 200-year-old masonry.*

2

2. *The large window openings on the long sides of the house and the skylights cut into the new thatched roof attest to a desire to provide maximum light in the large interior spaces.*

3. *The white paint, the French doors, and the elegant lamps betray the conversion of the rustic dwelling into a bourgeois retreat.*

3

4

5

4. *The dining room on the ground floor. The spare use of color, the rich materials, and the modern forms transform the interior as well from rusticity to elegance.*

5. *The huge bathroom accommodates a double-size sunken bathtub. The floor was raised by the height of two steps to create a platform for it.*

6. *As in all of the rooms, the ceiling, walls, and furnishings of the studio are white, permitting the countless art objects to stand out with their glowing colors.*

7. *The 1,600-square-foot living room on the ground floor is visually connected to the one above thanks to the large rectangular opening in the ceiling around the chimney.*

6

7

8. *A seating corner in the upstairs living room. The spiral staircase leads up to the sculpture loft.*

9. *Adjacent to the seating corner is a conference space. The door in the background leads to the guest room and servants' quarters.*

10. *Floor plans (ground floor, second floor, and lofts). Legend: 1 porch, 2 living room, 3 baths, 4 dining room, 5 kitchen, 6 studio, 7 living room, 8 storage, 9 servants' quarters, 10 guest room, 11 sleeping loft, 12 air space, 13 sculpture loft, 14 meditation room.*

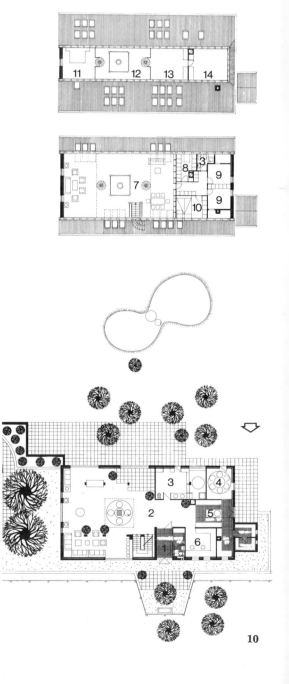

11. *View past the chimney opening toward the end of the living room with seating area and conference space. Above them are the sculpture loft and meditation room.*

12. *View from one loft to the other across the high upstairs living room. The owner's sleeping loft is in the background.*

11

12

7. CAREFULLY BROUGHT BACK TO LIFE

Renovation of a Baroque Manor House near Brussels, Belgium
Architect: René Stapels

When René Stapels discovered this estate in the vicinity of Brussels he could only guess at its former splendor, for it had badly deteriorated, and successive remodelings had covered most of its ceilings and columns. Once these had been exposed, it was clear that the manor house represents, not only for its size, but in its details as well, an outstanding example of rural architecture. Owned since the end of the Middle Ages by the Cistercian abbey of Villers, the complex was given its present form in 1755—the date is preserved in large iron numbers on the long wall of the barn. Shortly before the French Revolution the property had grown to encompass several hundred acres and employed as many as fifty people.

Four quite diverse buildings surround a large rectangle to which access is provided at two corners. Two of its sides are flanked by stalls and storerooms, the remaining two by the dwelling structure and the massive barn which, though sturdily built, required partial restoration. The size of the barn suggests that it was a tithe barn, accommodating not only the harvests of the farm itself but also contributions from the village destined for the abbey. Today the barn is no longer used, though on special occasions it is made available to the villagers for their traditional festivals.

In renovating the house structural changes were avoided as much as possible; only the installation of modern plumbing required certain alteration. Wherever practicable, new additions were placed free-standing so as to keep the structure visible. This principle is followed in the furnishings as well, which keep a respectable distance from the walls.

1. *Since the restoration the massive Baroque dignity of the large buildings enclosing a central courtyard can be fully appreciated even from a distance.*

1

2. *Wagons can enter the tithe barn from either end. Here the portions of the village harvest destined for the abbey were stored. On the courtyard side there is but a simple row of small windows and a single doorway, and the large expanse of unbroken wall sets the mood of the whole enclosure.*

3. *Access to the courtyard, which is enclosed on all four sides, is gained through entryways on diagonally opposite corners. The main entry is distinguished by a separate gatehouse.*

4, 5. *Just as in the structural restoration of the building, particular restraint was exercised in furnishings as well, so that architectural details are shown to best advantage. Here are the living room and dining room.*

4

5

6. *Floor plan (ground floor). Legend:*
1 entryway, 2 foyer, 3 closet, 4 living room, 5 studio,
6 bedroom, 7 bath, 8 guest room, 9 kitchen,
10 utility room, 11 dining room, 12 servants'
quarters, 13 washroom, 14 dog house, 15 stalls,
16 parking, 17 sheep barn, 18 barn, 19 garages.

7. *View of the kitchen, designed with up-to-
date technology for maximum convenience. The
attempt throughout the project to contrast new
built-ins and furnishings as much as possible
with the original architecture is especially
visible here.*

8, 9. *Even the bathrooms—here the master
bath—are arranged so that old and new are
distinctly separate.*

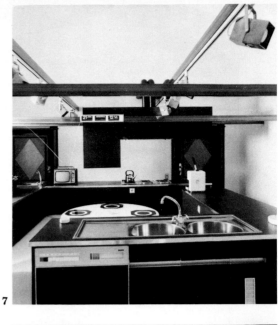

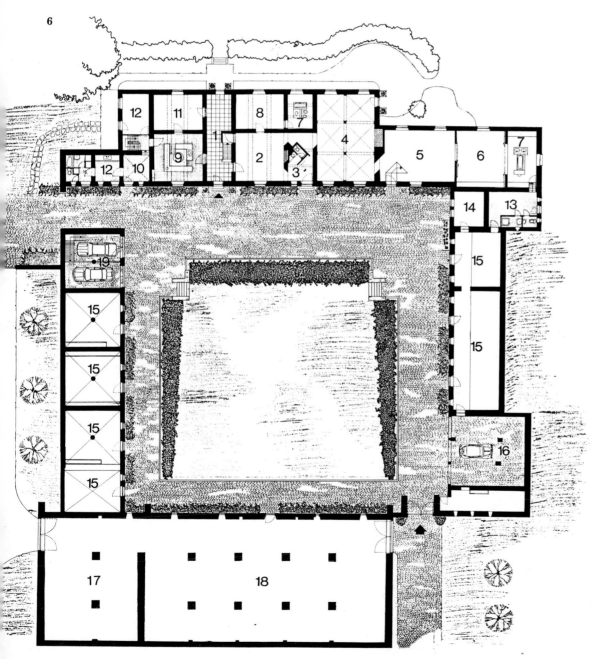

8. MORE ROOM IN THE SAME SPACE

Conversion and Expansion of a House on Falster Island, Denmark
Architects: Dissing + Weitling

The architects' challenge was to remodel a 130-year-old field worker's house measuring 650 square feet into a dwelling of 1,600 square feet without altering the structure's form and outline.

First 325 square feet of new space, used for bedrooms and a bath, were created in the attic. Another 625 square feet of additional space were achieved by means of an underground extension on the east side of the original structure, outfitted with a studio, a sauna, and a pantry. The outside walls of the subterranean extension were extended above the ground to form windbreaks on three sides, thus creating a courtyard in front of the existing house. Access into the extension is either by means of a stairway descending from the courtyard or through an underground corridor leading from the stairwell of the old structure.

A large opening was cut into the east wall of the courtyard in order to open the view across the adjacent fields and the distant landscape. Below this opening there is a narrow strip of skylights that bring sunlight into the studio.

The exterior treatment of the former field worker's house was typical of this part of Falster Island, and it was retained: a vertical covering of thatch over the half-timbering, secured by a lattice framework.

1. *Viewed from the west, the old farmhouse appears completely unchanged. The courtyard created above the underground addition extends to the east and is surrounded by walls one story high. Bedrooms and bath were built into the finished attic space.*

1

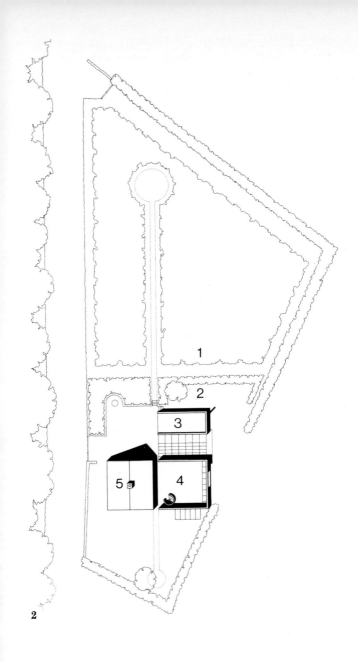

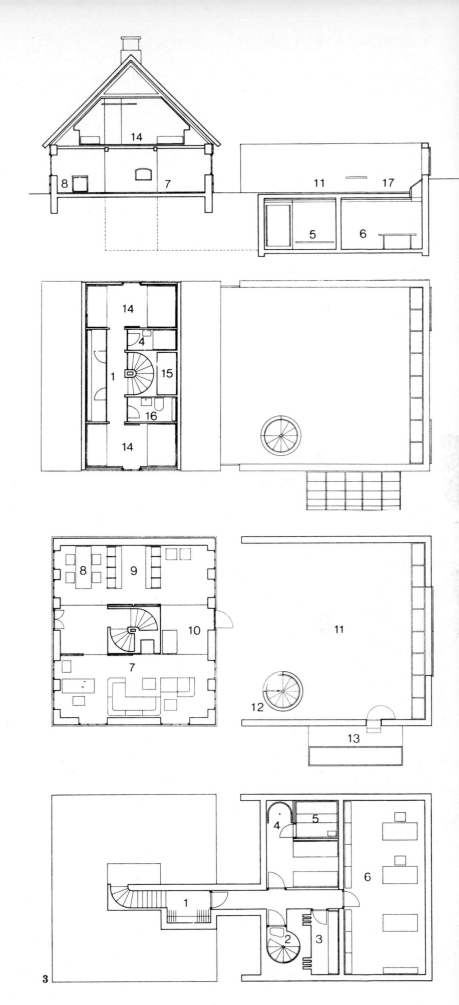

2. Site plan. Legend: 1 orchard, 2 vegetable garden, 3 garage and shop, 4 courtyard, 5 house.

3. Floor plans (underground level, ground floor, and second floor) and cross section. Legend: 1 closets, 2 stairway connecting courtyard and extension, 3 pantry, 4 showers, 5 sauna, 6 studio, 7 living room, 8 dining area, 9 kitchen, 10 entry, 11 courtyard, 12 top of stairway leading to extension, 13 greenhouse, 14 bedrooms, 15 equipment room, 16 bath.

4. *The central hallway on the upper floor. To the right are the descending staircase and the bathrooms, to the left closets, and in the background one of the two bedrooms.*

5. *Space limitations required that beds be placed under the eaves.*

6. *The ground-floor living room. The fireplace visible to the left is built into the central stairwell that connects all three levels.*

7. *The kitchen and dining area take up the remainder of the square ground floor of only 650 square feet.*

8. *View into the studio in the underground extension. The sole source of natural light is a strip of skylights on the east end.*

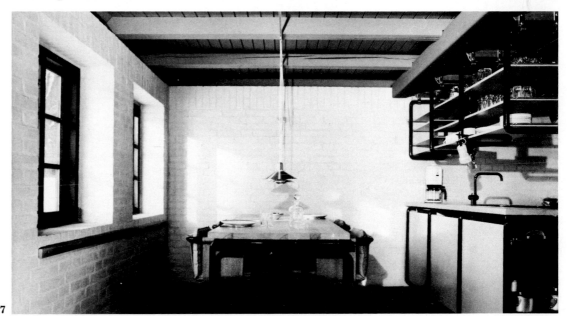

9. WITH A VIEW OF THE GREAT BELT

Conversion and Expansion of a Farmhouse in Drøsselbjerg, Zealand, Denmark
Architects: Dissing + Weitling

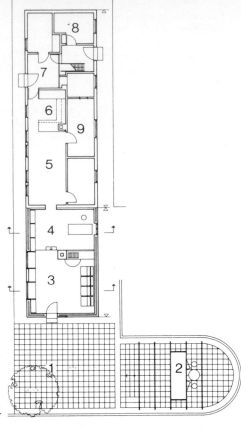

Two main considerations were faced by the architects in their expansion of this house set high above the Great Belt. On the one hand, the ceilings in the new living section were to be somewhat higher than those in the very cramped existing structure; also, the owners wished to have a special seating area with a view of the sea.

Greater room height was achieved not by sinking the floors but by raising the ceilings. The beams were repositioned higher between the rafters, creating the possibility of a curve between walls and ceiling. As for the second requirement, on the side of the house facing the sea deep cabinet walls were built, creating generous window seats. The windows themselves were enlarged in consideration of the view, raised well up into the area of the thatched roof, and rounded at the top, providing as well a neat solution to the problem of the roof overhang.

2

1. *Floor plan. Legend: 1 terrace, 2 toolshed, 3 living room, 4 workroom, 5 dining area, 6 kitchen, 7 porch, 8 bath, 9 bedroom.*

2. *The rounded windows extending right up into the roof permit even those seated well back in the room an optimal view of the sea.*

3. *Cross section through the addition.*

4. *View from the living room toward the Great Belt, the channel between Zealand and the mainland. On the seaward side of the house a cabinet wall was constructed, and the resulting deeper window recesses utilized as seating niches.*

5. *Room heights in the addition were increased so generously by raising the ceilings that the living room could be elevated by two steps.*

3

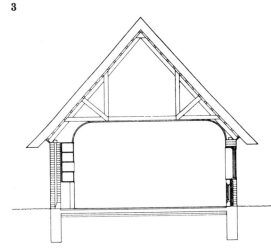

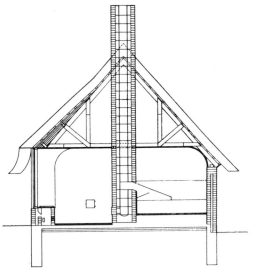

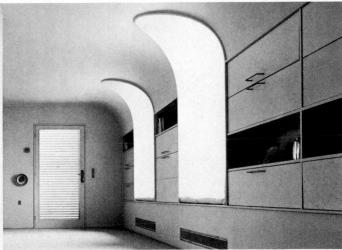

10. WOODEN SHED ON FIELDSTONE FOOTINGS

Conversion of a Barn near Burlington, Wisconsin, USA
Architects: Stanley Tigerman & Associates

The basic structure of the barn, at first glance not remotely promising, proved on closer inspection to be in good, solid condition. Thus it was possible to convert the structure into a vacation house for a couple and their four children without facing major problems. In order to preserve the barn's character as much as possible, it was decided to create an open arrangement of rooms from the floor to the roof, divided into various projecting levels connected to the main floor by means of a spiral stair and with each other by ramps. The silo that stood in front of the barn was given a new glass roof and a Franklin stove, and now serves as a meeting place for the family.

Unusual, but quite logical, approaches were taken with respect to design and technical problems. Wall openings were simply made wherever they were required; the arbitrary placement of windows permits one to guess the placement of interior levels even from the outside. The diagonal siding and paneling, running one way on the inside and the opposite way on the outside, are not only formally reasonable but structurally sound as well, for they strengthen the walls against the wind without additional bracing. All plumbing and conduits were left exposed and painted in bright colors so as to contrast with the walls.

1. *The exterior of the converted barn is characterized by its diagonal siding and by the arbitrary placement of windows. In front of the house is the glass roof of the former silo, which now serves as a family meeting place.*

1

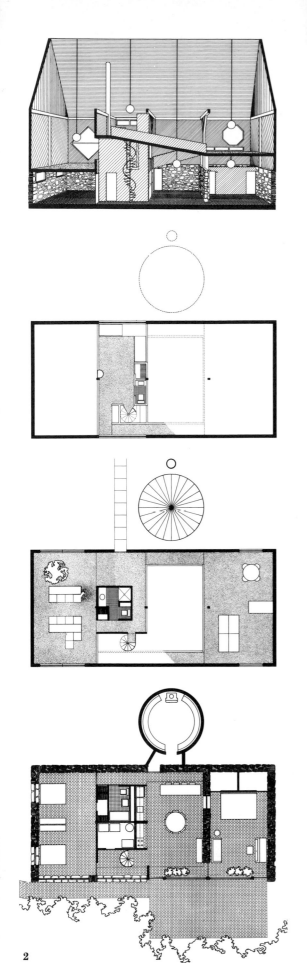

2. *Floor plans and perspective cross section.*

3. *The architecture of the family's meeting place is alive with contrasts. Above is the filigree of the glass roof, below the massive walls with exposed electrical conduit and a crudely cut entryway.*

4, 5. *In order to preserve the barn's open character as much as possible it was decided to treat the interior as a single space from floor to roof, divided into various projecting levels. The diagonal paneling plays up the planes of walls and balustrades, setting them off from the old post-and-beam construction and the modern technological additions.*

6. *Although the diagonal sheathing tends to minimize the division into single boards visually, causing the planes to function as units, the variety of texture and color in the wood prevents them from becoming monotonous. Here the kitchen and dining area with its generous wall of windows and its floor treatment extending out onto a terrace.*

4

5

11. BOSTON'S SKYLINE IN THE DISTANCE

Renovation of a Carriage House in Andover, Massachusetts, USA
Architects: Crissman & Solomon

In this renovation all changes were planned so that the west and south walls could be given over as much as possible to glass, making it feasible to enjoy to the full the splendid view of the surrounding country and even of Boston twenty-five miles away. To the north and east, where the turn-of-the-century building is attached to a barn, smaller window openings were retained, permitting an undisturbed transition to more traditional forms.

The task of the architects was to fit into the two floors—the cellar level is used as a garage—study space for the owner, a biologist, and a guest apartment that is totally self-sufficient. This guest suite was placed on the lower level and consists of a kitchen, bath, bedroom, and large living room with a projecting sundeck. The owner's quarters on the upper floor are connected to the lower living room by means of a gallery running along three of its sides and lighted to the west by a large semicircular window.

The whole exterior was covered with new cedar shingles, while the roof was left as it was. The floors merely required sanding.

1. *A large semicircular window frames the view of the surroundings from the second-floor gallery. A small sundeck projects from the living room on the lower level.*

1

2. *Floor plans (lower and upper levels). Legend: 1 sundeck, 2 living room, 3 bedroom, 4 dining area, 5 kitchen, 6 barn, 7 reading area, 8 study, 9 bedroom.*

3. *The house before renovation. The roof remains unchanged, but the exterior walls were given new cedar shingles.*

4. *Windows placed so as to capture maximum light and view were set into the walls with a minimum of framing, so that the visual transition from inside to outside is as simple as possible.*

3

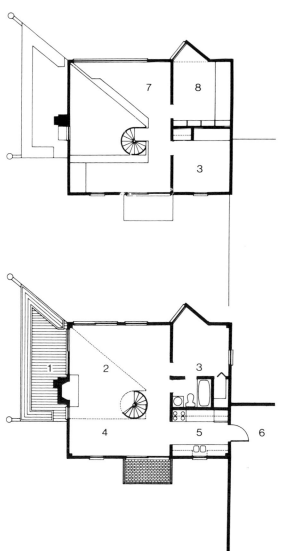

2

4

5

5. *View from the gallery of the distant landscape through the new, large semicircular window.*

6. *The owner's study, accessible from the reading area on the gallery.*

7. *The living room on the lower floor. To the left, the sharp angle of the sundeck projects into the landscape. A portion of the semicircular window is visible above the gallery's balustrade.*

6

12. FORMAL SPLENDOR IN AN ENCHANTED WILDERNESS

Renovation of a House near Darmstadt, West Germany
Architect: Theodor Seifert

Habitable space of 7,000 square feet and ceilings 11 1/2 feet high convinced the architect, in spite of his professional urges, to forego building a new house for himself and settle for a renovated one. He only occupies one floor himself, to be sure, with an area of only 1,900 square feet. By means of deft apportionment of the remaining space he made room for seven tenants as well in the vintage 1913 villa. Essentially the rooms on the owner's floor remain as they were; only their functions are changed. The glassed-in veranda became a dining room, the former hallway is now a comfortable sitting room with fireplace, and the old, overly spacious kitchen has shrunk to a rather more modern size. The kitchen has been compensated for in this reduction by being fitted out with every modern convenience, reducing considerably the burdens of housework.

The guiding principle in all the planning was to preserve as much as possible the atmosphere of the stately house; questions of function were given second place. The surroundings, of exceptional loveliness and savored by the owner on his morning ride to the estate's boundaries and beyond, were to be enjoyed from as many rooms as possible. To this end the living room and bedroom flow into one another, thus preserving in quite a new way the original feeling of the house. As a result, square footage for these two rooms has been kept at a minimum—one of the reasons these 1,900 square feet provide more usable space than usual.

1. *Even after renovation and conversion into eight apartments the pre-World War I villa continues to be a dramatically imposing structure. The owner occupies the main floor only.*

1

2. *Floor plan (main floor). Legend:*
1 stairwell, 2 living room, 3 living areas,
4 sleeping area, 5 dining room, 6 terrace,
7 child's room, 8 bath, 9 guest room, 10 kitchen.

3. *The lot is as large as a park, with more than an acre of land. Since the plants have been growing wild for decades the garden has reverted to the character of a natural landscape.*

4. *The original front doors of the house were replaced by glass ones. The former entry steps now serve as a terrace.*

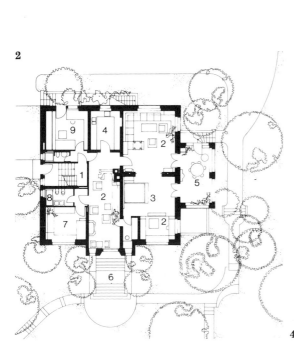

57

5. *The wood paneling in the living room was removed, and the walls painted white. The double doors, however, as well as the large windows and the original ceiling serve to maintain its formal character.*

6. *The bedroom lies between two living areas, with which it forms a visual and functional unit. The door in the background leads to a storeroom.*

5

6

7. *The smaller of the two living areas. It is raised slightly above the level of the bedroom.*

8. *Dinner is being served today next to the imposing round windows of the veranda. The dining room's magnificent view compensates for its distance from the kitchen.*

13. SWIMMING AT THE EDGE OF THE WOODS

Renovation and Expansion of a House in Randers, East Jutland, Denmark
Architects: Nils Primdahl and Erich Weitling

The owner of this 1965 house wanted more space for relaxation and entertaining as well as an indoor swimming pool. At the same time, the existing villa was to be rearranged so that the children's rooms and those of the adults were more clearly separated.

The original house was built as a long low building parallel to a gentle slope. Thus it was simple to make the addition two stories high, sinking the lower one into the ground. In the upper floor of the addition there is a large living room leading directly into the old one, while the lower floor is given over to the pool. Extending out from the pool is a small sundeck that borders directly on the woods.

The exteriors of the original structure and the new one blend well in spite of their different treatment. This was achieved primarily by the use of the same roof angle on the addition as on the original house.

1, 2. Despite their different exterior treatment the original house and the new extension harmonize well, largely thanks to the adoption for the new structure of the roof angle of the older one.

1

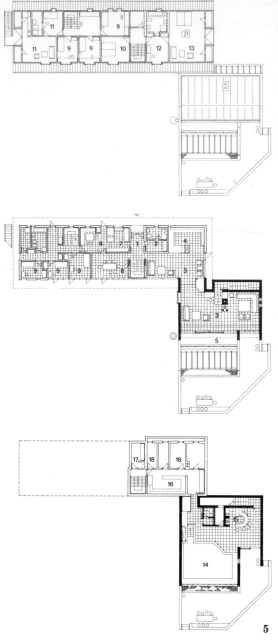

3

4

5

3, 4. *The large living room in the addition is characterized by the big ceramic tiles on the floor, the whitewashed masonry, and the exposed wooden girders supporting the roof.*

5. *Floor plans (lower level, ground floor, and second floor). Legend: 1 entry, 2 closet, 3 living rooms, 4 TV room, 5 balcony, 6 breakfast area, 7 kitchen, 8 dining room, 9 children's rooms, 10 guest room, 11 servants' rooms, 12 dressing room, 13 master bedroom, 14 pool, 15 bar, 16 utility room, 17 sauna, 18 storerooms.*

6. *The pool and bar on the lower level of the addition. On the left is a door to the outside and the peaceful, tree-edged sundeck.*

14. TRANSPARENCY IN STEEL AND GLASS

Enlargement of a House in Hasseris, North Jutland, Denmark
Architect: Jacob Blegvad

In charming contrast to the stodginess of this turn-of-the-century villa, a glass cage was constructed in a form resembling a folded caterpillar—but one that poses no threat to the garden surroundings. On one side it shelters a swimming pool, and on the other a fireplace and dining area, the whole filled with luxuriant plants. A sauna, bath, and changing rooms are contained in the masonry core. The delicate, transparent structure consists of a steel skeleton supporting a double layer of thermal glass. The foundations and the swimming pool were cast in concrete.

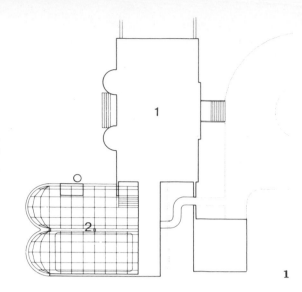

1

2

1. *Site plan. Legend: 1 main building, 2 extension.*

2. *The glass caterpillar forms a pleasant contrast to the massiveness of the villa from the turn of the century. By covering the addition completely with glass the architect prevented it from competing visually with the existing structure.*

3. *Floor plan (ground floor) and cross section of the addition. Legend: 1 conservatory, 2 pool, 3 sauna, 4 shower, 5 toilet, 6 changing room.*

4, 5. *The abundance of glass allows interior and exterior views to run together. The owners of the traditional stone house can here enjoy a totally different architectural experience.*

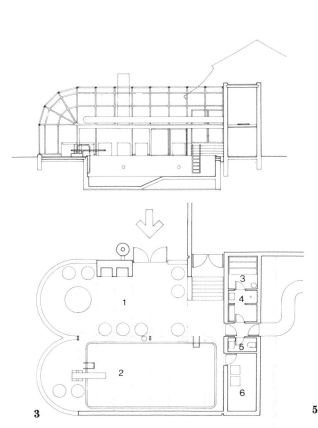

15. FROM BILLIARD ROOM TO SWIMMING POOL

Renovation and Expansion of a House in London, England
Architects: Ted Levy, Benjamin & Partners

The unusually commodious house with its long interior vistas and its aura of the good old days, typical as it is of large numbers of homes built before the turn of the century, does not at first betray the functional reorganization of rooms that a comparison of floor plans reveals. Dominating the ground floor is a large swimming pool in what was formerly the billiard room, expanded for the purpose by means of an extension toward the garden. This extension is completely encased in glass, with doors that open onto the terrace. A self-sufficient bachelor apartment for the oldest son occupies the remainder of this level. Above, on the main floor, are a central hall, a living room, a billiard and dining room, adjacent kitchen and pantries, and a small TV room in which the youngest child may also do his homework. The next level comprises a library on a landing of the central stairs and the younger children's bedrooms. From the library a spiral stair leads up to the parents' sun-filled bedroom and studio suite.

The imposing style of the house, with its generous dimensions and sensible arrangement of spaces, is complemented by selective use of materials: from the pale blue glass tiles of the swimming pool to the wool broadloom carpeting and the carved walnut feet of the billiard table.

1. *View from the northwest. Behind the second gable from the right is the stairwell that descends to a large central hall on the main floor. A glassed conservatory is adjacent to it.*

2. *Floor plans (ground level, main floor, second floor, and third floor). Legend: 1 living rooms, 2 changing room, 3, sauna, 4 pool, 5 kitchens, 6 baths, 7 bedrooms, 8 furnace room, 9 hall, 10 TV room, 11 utility room, 12 dining room, 13 library, 14 toilet, 15 guest room, 16 bed-sitting room, 17 servants' quarters, 18 gallery, 19 dressing rooms, 20 studio, 21 terrace, 22 master bedroom.*

3. *On the south side the lower floor is mainly above ground level, so that it was possible to surround the pool with large glass windows on three sides. On the left, next to the stairs, a portion of the glass roof over the pool is visible.*

4. *View of the swimming pool. The strip windows in the roof on the south and west sides help considerably to make the space seem light and open.*

1

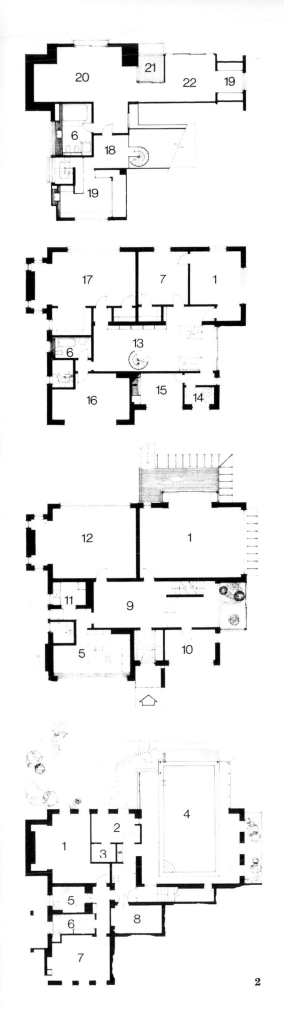

3

4

5. *The dining room on the main floor also houses the displaced billiard table.*

6. *The living room on the main floor. It sits directly above the former billiard room, which now houses the ground-floor pool.*

5

6

7

7. *The complex junctions of roof planes at the top of the irregular house give the rooms on the third floor a special character, one not at all comparable to that of the usual garret apartment.*

8. *View from the gallery into the library. In the background is the central stairway leading down into the hall.*

8

16. ADAPTING TO THE DIMENSIONS OF THE BILLIARD ROOM

Expansion of a House in London, England
Architect: Christopher Bowerbank

The rather modest original house was built in the middle of the last century, but shortly before 1900 it was enlarged by the addition of an 18×36 foot billiard room with elegant wood paneling, long since used simply as a living room. The present owner wished to add another floor to this one-story addition, on the one hand creating space for another bedroom that could double as a studio, and on the other hand lessening the contrast between the quite unequal wings of the house.

The new space consists first of an entryway at the top of the stairs with an octagonal pointed roof above it, the outline of which is reflected in the pattern of the floor. Next comes a large bathroom that has access by means of a corridor between the landing and the new bedroom to a small walled terrace. The bedroom itself is remarkable not only for its size, but because the exposed beams of the hip roof are supported by slender wooden pillars.

The new exterior walls are broken by double French doors opening onto a small balcony on the south side, with a semicircular window extending up into the roof above it, and on the east side by a small bay window.

1. *Only the lack of a London patina on the new bricks betrays that an addition was recently made here. On the new floor above a former billiard room, which had functioned as a living room for years, space was created for an additional bedroom and studio, a bath with its own nearby terrace, and an octagonal stair landing and entryway.*

1

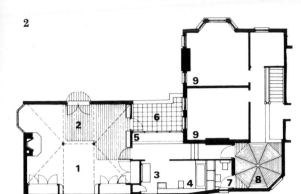

2

3

2. Floor plan. Legend: 1 sleeping area,
2 studio area, 3 dressing area, 4 bath, 5 planting
boxes, 6 terrace, 7 toilet, 8 entryway, 9 existing
bedrooms.

3. The terrace outside the corridor between
the entryway at the top of the stairs and the
combination studio and bedroom. To the left
are windows with planting boxes along the
corridor, next to them the door into the new
bedroom.

4. View down the corridor into the new
bedroom and studio. To the right are the
windows opening onto the terrace, to the left
the dressing area.

4

5

5. *In the combined bedroom and studio the two functions are located on different levels, their boundaries marked by the two slender wooden pillars that support the open-beamed ceiling. These structural elements give the room its informal character.*

6. *The landing at the top of the stairs is surmounted by an octagonal pointed roof, the shape of which is repeated in the flooring.*

7. *View from the bath out into the corridor with its planting boxes and windows opening on the terrace.*

6

7

8.   *The bedroom and studio. The closed door
to the left leads to the terrace, the open one in
the center to the corridor and bath.*

17. GROWTH BY CELL DIVISION

Renovation and Expansion of a House in Chevy Chase, Maryland, USA
Architect: Hugh Newell Jacobsen

The older portion of this building was erected in 1871 as an addition to a larger country house long since torn down. Its original character had been significantly obscured through the years by the application of turquoise paint, new window frames, and a fake wrought-iron porch.

In enlarging the house, the architect restored the existing building essentially to its original condition, then placed alongside it a mirror-image copy, tying the two together with a glassed entryway. To make the mirror effect even more striking, he added fully glassed-in bays on the south sides of the identical wings, which together with still another bay window on the long side of the extension expand the interior visually.

The new structure houses a spacious living room on the ground floor, and on the upper floor a bedroom nearly as large with its own bath and toilet.

Though great restraint was exercised in the design of the exterior, the interior is marked with the architect's signature throughout. It is precisely the contrast between the Victorian exterior, preserved out of consideration for the surrounding neighborhood, and the classical modernity of the interiors that gives the house its unique charm.

1. *The original character of the house had been considerably compromised by the addition of a coat of turquoise paint, new window frames, and a fake wrought-iron porch.*

1

2. *Site plan.*

3. *The renovation restored the earlier clean lines of the building. By stressing the window frames, corner moldings, sills, and eaves, the architect achieved an effect of extreme discipline. The house appears scarcely larger than it was before, though the entryway in the connecting structure and the entire right wing are new.*

4. *The west side of the new addition, which contains a spacious living room on the ground floor, and a bedroom of nearly equal size, bath, and toilet on the floor above.*

3

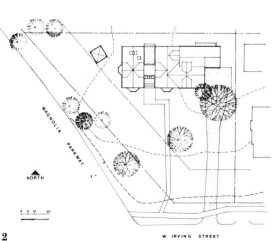

2

NORTH

W. IRVING STREET

4

5. *The bath and toilet on the second floor of the addition.*

6. *Floor plans (ground floor and second floor). Legend: 1 living room, 2 music room, 3 playroom, 4 kitchen, 5 dining room, 6 baths, 7 bedrooms.*

7. *The living room in the ground floor of the addition is much airier than its exterior would lead one to suspect. Though the architect worked with strictest discipline on the outside of the house, the interiors bear his personal stamp throughout.*

5   6

18. LARGER INSIDE THAN OUT

Renovation of a House in Nyack, New York, USA
Architect: James R. Lamantia

The house was built in the 1880's by the balloon-frame method typical of buildings of its kind in that era. While it was left largely unchanged on the exterior, the interior was completely renovated in accordance with the wishes of the present owner, a painter. A two-story living room was created by removing the floors in a fourth of the house. At the same time a bearing wall was removed and replaced by wooden beams supported by posts placed behind the two brick chimneys. In order to prevent the resulting spaces—still none too large—from appearing even smaller, only the bathrooms were fully enclosed. Other rooms flow easily into each other. Wherever possible, the original floors were preserved, merely sanded and waxed.

In spite of the necessary replacement of old plumbing and wiring, the architect managed to keep the cost of renovation extremely low.

Especially successful in this house is the choice of furnishings, which in their simplicity have a modest and charming effect.

1. *The downstairs now comprises the owner's studio, a dining area, kitchen, and utility room. A straight flight of stairs above the dining area leads up to the entry level.*

2. *Axonometric projection.*

1

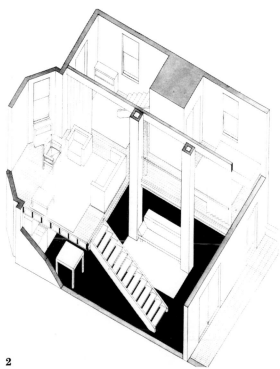

2

3. *Floor plans (lower level, entry floor, second floor). Legend: 1 gallery, 2 dining area, 3 kitchen, 4 utility room, 5 gallery, 6 air space, 7 living quarters, 8 toilet, 9 sleeping areas, 10 bath.*

4. *The entry floor. On the left, a stairway leading to the second floor; to the right, behind a living-room sofa, the air space above the lower level.*

5. *View from the studio into the living area. Below, the kitchen and dining areas.*

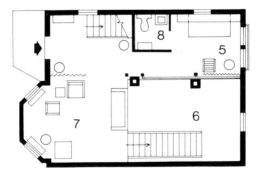

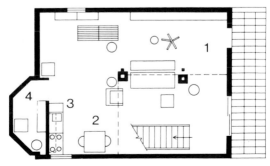

19. RELEASE FROM PERPETUAL GLOOM

Renovation and Expansion of a House in Essex, Connecticut, USA
Architects: Moore, Grover, Harper

The architects' assignment in this case was to create out of an assortment of small, dark, chopped-up rooms a bright expanse of space, and to give the owners the chance to enjoy their splendid view of the harbor and the banks of the Connecticut River.

The entire interior of the 1840 house was gutted, making possible a largely open arrangement of rooms on all three floors, with vertical and diagonal views that make the house appear larger than it is. A two-story extension houses a kitchen and dining area on its upper floor, and a studio and bath below.

The exterior remains essentially unchanged and blends unobtrusively with the neighboring architecture. A brick chimney was built on one of the gable ends, and an old deck was replaced by a new one. The new windows on the river side have large panes, but elsewhere they were made to resemble the old ones with their characteristic mullions.

In spite of all of its changes, the interior corresponds nicely to the exterior, largely because the designers did not refrain from treating the spaces sculpturally, subtly coordinating their division and arrangement.

1. *View of the house from the street. A new chimney was built on this end, and next to it is a woodbin accessible from both inside and out.*

1

2. *Floor plans (lower level, entry level, and second floor). Legend: 1 studio, 2 baths, 3 music room, 4 bedrooms, 5 kitchen, 6 dining area, 7 air space, 8 entry, 9 living room, 10 deck.*

3, 4. *The garden side of the house. On the left is the new two-story extension, with kitchen and dining area on the upper level, and studio and bath below.*

3

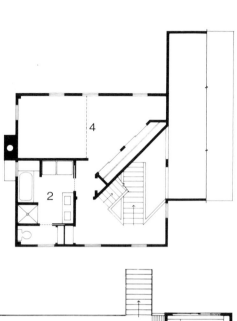

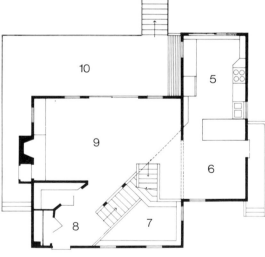

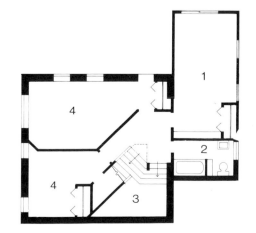

2

4

5. *View of the harbor from the dining area.*

6. *The living room occupies nearly the whole entry level of the original structure. On the left, next to the fireplace, is the door to the woodbin, which looks from the street like a birdhouse.*

7. *The whole interior of the 1840 house was removed, making it possible to create an open arrangement of rooms through all three levels.*

8. *The staircase forms the design focus for the entire house. A flight of angular steps leads up from the lower level to an in-between landing and onto the entry level (right).*

9. *The stairway leading from the entry level to the second floor. The diagonal partitions and balconies create numerous conjunctions that give the interior space the feeling of sculpture.*

20. GOLD RUSH FALSE FRONT

Renovation and Expansion of a House in Palo Alto, California, USA
Architects: MLTW/Turnbull Associates

The owners were attracted to this 1930's house primarily for its site, but wished to enlarge it to accommodate a studio and an additional bedroom, and to reorganize the existing spaces so as to make them better suited to an informal lifestyle.

The addition lies behind a closed, partially false front. It is attached to the narrow street side of the original house and contains a studio on the ground floor and a bedroom above. The basis for this decision was the wish to remove the entryway from the old house. It now extends like a corridor alongside the new studio. This increased the space in the original house, and the architects were able to create a bazaarlike variety of spatial impressions as one proceeds through the rooms.

1. *The house before renovation. The addition with its false front was placed between the house and the garage.*

1

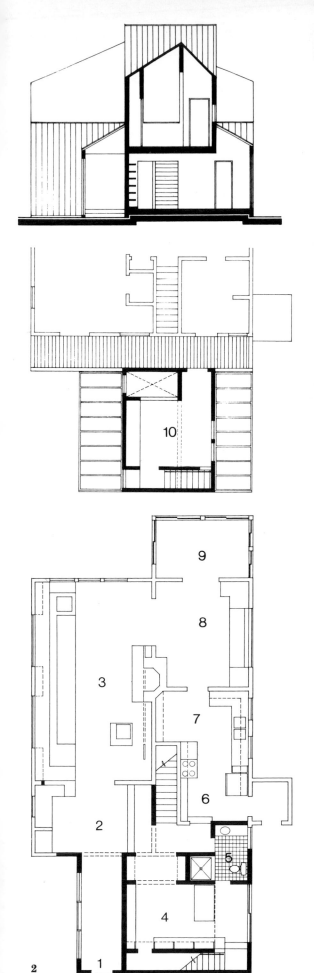

2. *Floor plans (ground floor and second floor)
and cross section. Legend: 1 entryway, 2 foyer,
3 living room, 4 studio, 5 bath, 6 kitchen,
7 breakfast area, 8 dining room, 9 veranda,
10 bedroom.*

3. *The extension houses, in addition to the
entryway pulled out from the old house, a
studio on the ground floor and a bedroom
above.*

4

4. View of the kitchen with its walls displaying a collection of baskets of every variety.

5. The studio on the ground floor of the addition opens onto the garden through wide glass doors. In the background, the first step of a landing is visible, from which a stairway leads to the upper level.

5

6. *View from the studio of the new false-front gable wall, which is covered with vertical siding on the outside. The large vase stands on the landing of the stairway leading to the second story.*

7. *The new bedroom on the upper level of the addition. The stairs lead down behind the white partition that forms the headboard of the bed.*

8. *Lining up the living room, foyer, and entryway produced a long vista with an unusual impression of spaciousness.*

21. VIEWING DOME ON THE ROOF

Renovation and Expansion of a Vacation House in Westhampton Beach, New York,
  USA
Architect: Ari Bahat

An unimposing summer house was to be enlarged as inexpensively as possible so as to make it usable the whole year. The small plot and the marvelous view suggested expansion upward from the single-story structure.

The ground floor was expanded by means of two additional rooms into a square with one slightly beveled corner. A platform was then constructed above the whole, right on top of the old, nearly flat roof. The roof and platform were hidden behind a frieze on all four sides, the paneling of which serves in places as a balustrade for the sundeck. A geodesic dome was set on top of the platform, one constructed of wood and aluminum with a sheathing of insulated plates. From inside, one ascends to the dome by means of a spiral stair from the lower hall; from outside, a diagonal staircase leads up to the sundeck.

In order to block the view into the lower rooms from the street the architect erected a screen in front of the south side of the house. Its arrow-shape causes the passerby to be in doubt about its true purpose. The exterior walls of the ground floor were neutralized by means of a coat of dark gray paint, so that the lighter frieze and the white dome above would stand out more clearly.

1. *Before renovation the vacation house resembled nothing so much as an army barracks.*

2. *A platform was placed on top of the existing structure, braced above the original, gently sloping roof. The roof and platform were then wrapped with a vertical frieze, and a geodesic dome placed on the resulting sundeck.*

1

2

3

3. *In order to prevent passersby from seeing into the ground-floor rooms, the architect placed a screen in front of the exposed south side of the house. Its arrow-shape leaves some doubt about its true function.*

4. *The living room, dining area, and kitchen are housed in the geodesic dome on the platform. The decagon has a diameter of roughly twenty-four feet.*

4

5. One of the ground-floor bedrooms.

6. Floor plans (ground floor and upper level).
Legend: 1 entry area, 2 studio, 3 bedrooms,
4 baths, 5 living room, 6 dining area, 7 kitchen,
8 deck.

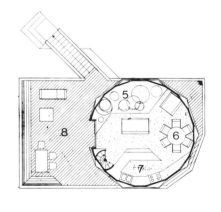

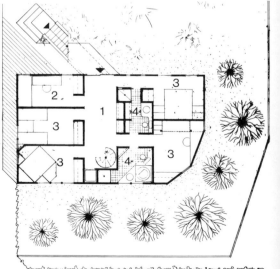

5

6

7, 8. *The dome is constructed of triangular facets, some of which are partially or wholly composed of glass. These glass surfaces are distributed in different shapes and heights.*

9. *View of the water through the living-room windows.*

7

8

9

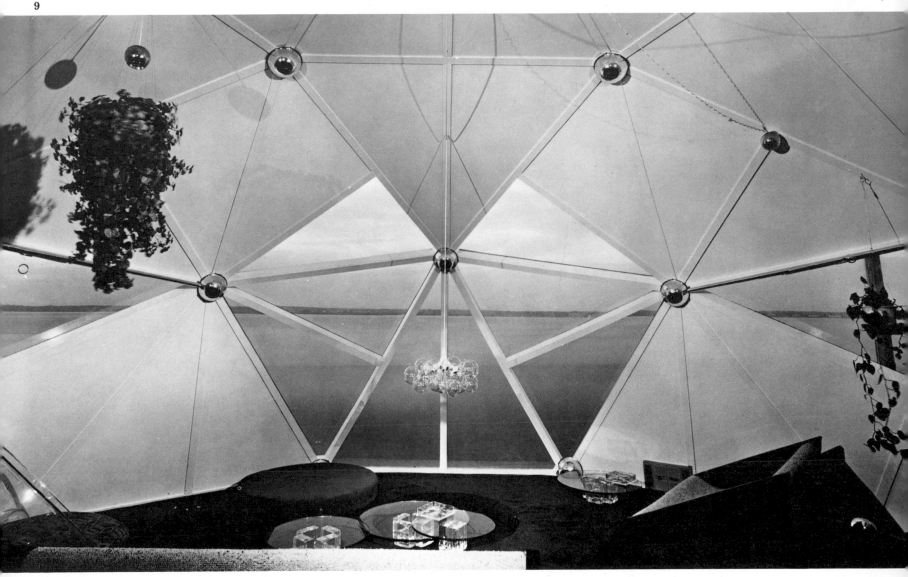

22. EAST AND WEST IN HARMONY

Restoration and Expansion of a House in Sidi Bou Saïd, Tunisia
Architects: Eric and Elda Hoechel

This structure, which now houses two apartments and a small office, is said to have been built as the guest house of a small nineteenth-century palace. The northern section around the courtyard was well preserved, while the adjacent west wing had been largely destroyed; the southern section was in terrible condition.

The surviving portions of the house were restored, though somewhat freely to be sure and with an eye to the new space requirements. The remaining sections are completely new, as is obvious from the frequent use of curved walls and deliberately unexpected details such as the rounded glass doors. The freer new forms are strikingly well suited to the older context.

Living areas are located on the ground floor, sleeping areas above. A small swimming pool has been installed in the common garden.

1. *View from the garden of the living area in the northern section of the house. This section is new, as the abundant use of curved walls and rounded glass doors attests.*

1

2. *View from the courtyard of the north-wing living section. The two-story section of the house is behind the viewer.*

3. *From the courtyard, a narrow staircase leads up to the sundeck. An open fireplace is set against the wall.*

4. *Floor plans (ground floor and second floor). Legend: 1 dwelling entry, 2 office entry, 3 toilet, 4 living room, 5 reading corner, 6 fireplace corner, 7 dining rooms, 8 kitchens, 9 furnace room, 10, 11 reception areas, 12 office, 13 drafting room, 14 archives, 15 card room, 16 storeroom, 17 pool, 18 baths, 19 bedrooms.*

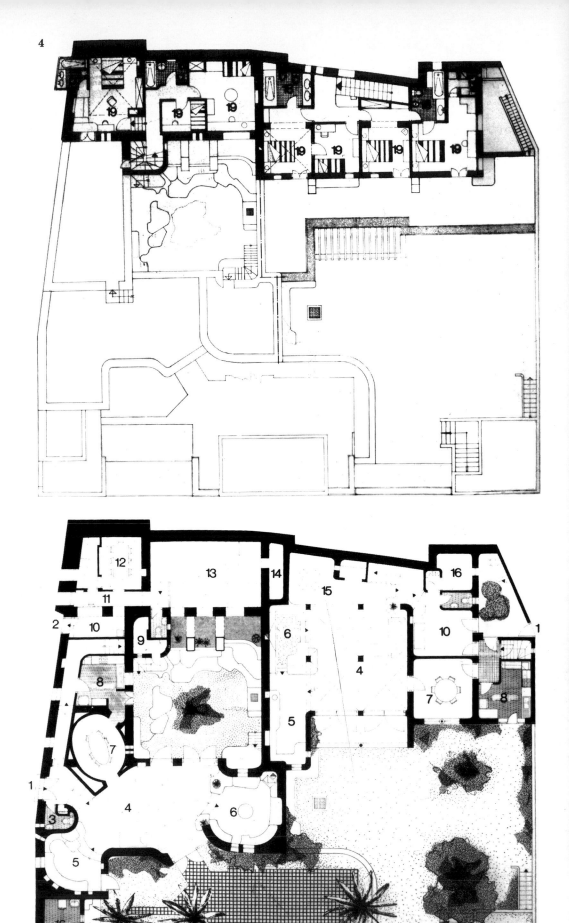

5, 6. *The fireplace corner in the living room of the north wing of the house is elevated by two steps. As in other rooms, it is furnished only partially with moveable seating. The fireplace, the broad steps, and the built-in benches, together with the wall openings, form a sculptural whole.*

7. *View of the north-wing living room. The enclosed atrium is on the left; the glass door on the right leads to the garden.*

23. NEW ROOMS IN ANCIENT HOUSING

Renovation of an Apartment in Portovenere, Liguria, Italy
Architect: Arturo Belloni

Tightly packed medieval houses, only 10–12 feet wide but 45–50 feet deep, generally seven stories high, their lower floors cut into the steep cliffs at the back, their front doors only a few steps from the water—this is the protected heritage of architecture along the shoreline in Portovenere on Italy's Gulf of La Spezia on the Ligurian Sea.

The apartment we show comprises two stories with a view of the sea. The back of the house appears to be at ground level and it is here that one enters it. Kitchen and living spaces were located on the upper floor, the lower one was set aside for bedrooms and bath.

The interiors are alive with contrast between the elegant modern furnishings and the existing structure, whose most unusual proportions were left unchanged.

1. *The shoreline at Portovenere on the Gulf of La Spezia presents a tightly packed front of medieval houses no more than 10–12 feet wide but 45–50 feet deep.*

1

2

3

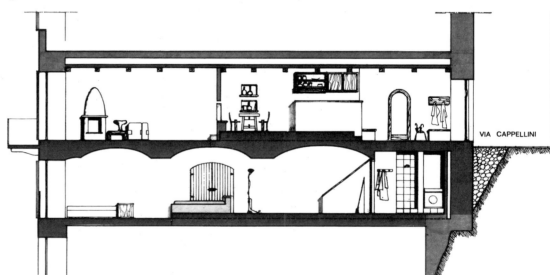

VIA CAPPELLINI

VIA CAPPELLINI

2. The entrances to the houses line a narrow alley along the back. The apartment illustrated is in number 89.

3. View of the house facades from the water. The renovated apartment occupies the second and third floors above the Bar Gelateria Babani; its windows are above the word "Babani."

4. Floor plans and cross section. The sleeping area is on the lower floor, the living area above.

4

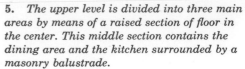

5. The upper level is divided into three main areas by means of a raised section of floor in the center. This middle section contains the dining area and the kitchen surrounded by a masonry balustrade.

6. By the window, a smalll seating area was placed near the fireplace. The window opens onto a narrow balcony from which one can view the harbor and the open sea.

7. View from the dining area toward the living room.

8. The kitchen is raised an additional two steps above the dining area.

9. A steep stairway leads down to the sleeping area on the lower level. A series of iron rings takes the place of a banister.

10. The bath is the only fully enclosed room in the whole apartment.

11. View across the bed toward the stairs leading up to the living area and the door to the bath. The large door on the left hides a recessed wardrobe.

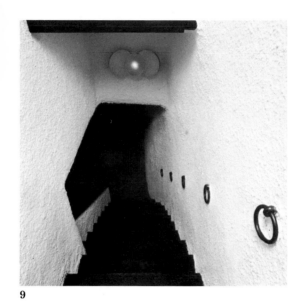

9

10

11

24. TORN DOWN AND PUT BACK TOGETHER AGAIN

Renovation of a House in Berne, Switzerland
Architect: Frank Geiser

Berne's building ordinances rigorously protect the street facades in the old city and prescribe the architectural style of its buildings. In renovating this house in the Nydeggstalden there could thus be no thought of dramatic architectural changes; only the function of the building could be improved.

Within a period of ten months the derelict old structure was removed and a new building exactly like it erected. Certain elements were preserved, for example the entry door and the roof tiles, which were all replaced in their original positions. Behind the reconstructed sandstone facade reinforced concrete floors, covered in each apartment by carpeting, now stretch between the renovated fire walls. The original number of apartments was kept, with four one-room studios and five two-room dwellings distributed among the building's main floors. New are an apartment with a gallery on the top floor, and a gallery and exhibition space in part of the ground floor and the second story. In the subbasement are a guard room, cellars, boiler and duct rooms, and the motor room for the newly installed elevator.

Because of the narrow facades—only thirteen feet on the Nydeggstalden front and twenty-six feet facing the Aare River—it was decided to place the open kitchens and the bathrooms in the middle of each floor, each with its own ventilation to the roof.

1. *Views of the house from the Nydeggstalden (left) and from the Aare River (right).*

2. *View of the house from the Nydeggstalden. The curve of the street occasioned pie-shaped building sites, so that the fronts of the buildings are extremely narrow.*

1

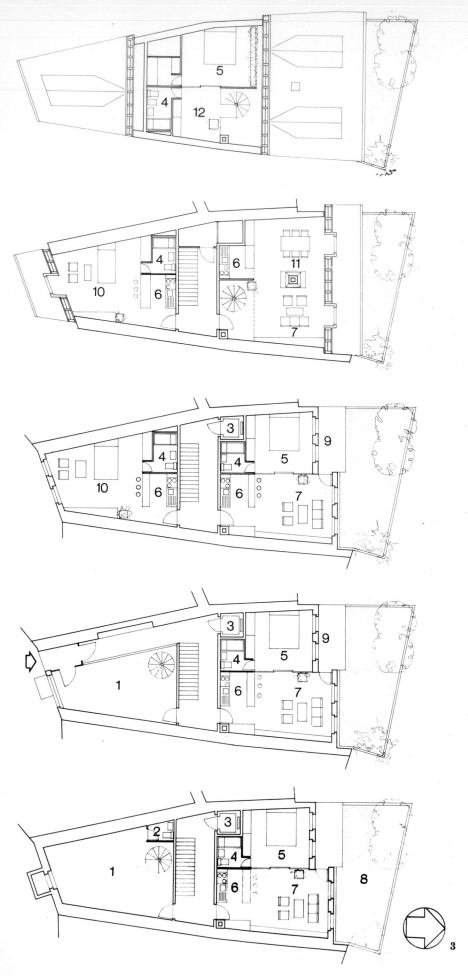

3. *Floor plans (basement, ground floor, second, third, and fourth stories). Legend: 1 gallery, 2 toilet, 3 elevator, 4 baths, 5 bedrooms, 6 kitchens, 7 living rooms, 8 garden, 9 arbors, 10 bed-sitting room, 11 dining area, 12 study.*

4. *View of the living room of the top-floor apartment from a gallery reached by means of a spiral stair. At the very top are the bedroom and a study.*

Reconstruction of a Bourgeois Mansion in Cologne, West Germany
Architect: Friedrich Wilhelm Kraemer

This mansion, built in the first third of the last century, was destroyed in the last weeks of World War II, and it stood as a ruin in the center of Cologne until someone was found who was willing to rebuild it in accordance with rather rigid landmark restrictions.

Reconstruction was essentially like building a new structure, for only the outside walls were remaining above ground level. There was no attempt to duplicate precisely the original mansion; on the contrary, rather significant changes were made. The ground-floor ceiling is now considerably higher, for example, making space for a mezzanine. The arrangement of rooms is completely new, and, in addition to the dormers on the roof, a large gabled penthouse was constructed, perfectly in keeping with the Neo-Classical facade on the front, but modern on the side facing the garden. A totally new office building was constructed as an extension on the garden side. Built largely of glass and steel, it includes a basement parking garage and a terrace with luxuriant plantings on the roof.

The removal of old partitions and layers of plaster in the cellar exposed a double-vaulted chamber which was once part of a thirteenth-century Franciscan monastery. The room now serves as an art gallery. The enlarged top floor of the mansion contains the architect's own apartment.

1. *View across the new addition into the atrium. The steeply slanted glass roofs create a smooth transition between old and new, and they cause the rather cramped atrium to appear larger than it is.*

2, 3. *The garden side and street facade of the reconstructed mansion. The large gabled structure centered in the roof has been treated in the Neo-Classical manner on the street side, but has a very modern appearance on the side facing the garden.*

1

2

3

4. *Floor plans (basement level, ground floor, mezzanine, second floor, and top floor) and cross section. Legend: 1 garage, 2 art gallery, 3 equipment rooms, 4 secretarial offices, 5 refreshment room, 6 entry hall, 7 glass roof, 8 garage entrance, 9 offices, 10 rest room, 11 roof terrace, 12 consultation rooms, 13 archives, 14 kitchen, 15 conference room, 16 guest room, 17 kitchen and utility room, 18 living and dining area, 19 library, 20 bedroom.*

4

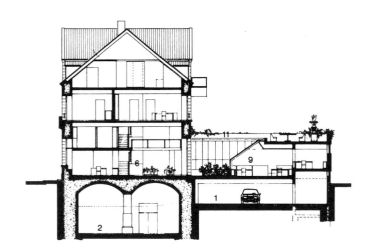

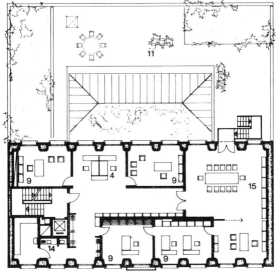

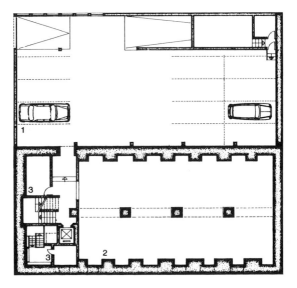

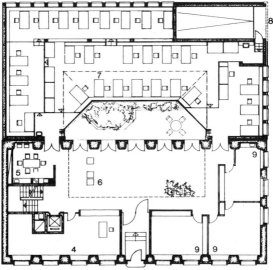

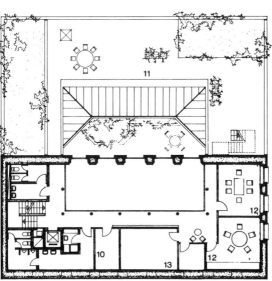

5. *View from the top-floor living room out through the wall of glass on the garden side.*

6. *The library in the architect's apartment. The right-angle book wall separates the reading area visually.*

7. *The apartment living room looking in the direction of the street. A balcony spans the room above the dining area.*

8

8. *The large entry hall opens onto the atrium through five large French doors. By raising the ground-floor ceiling in the reconstruction it was possible to introduce a mezzanine accessible from a balcony running along three sides of the room.*

9. *A double-vaulted cellar was exposed during reconstruction. Once part of a thirteenth-century Franciscan monastery, it now functions as an art gallery.*

9

10, 11. *The drafting room of the architect's offices in the new addition.*

10

11

Renovation and Expansion of a Corner Row House in Cologne, West Germany
Architects: Planning Group BOS—Ulrich Böttger, Klaus Orlich, and Peter Sandleben

The original structure from 1929, in spite of being a row house with all the features associated with such dwellings, had truly princely dimensions. During renovation it was given even more space by adding an extension containing a four-car garage on the ground level and a swimming pool, sauna, and storeroom below.

As one might suspect, given its size, the building serves a number of functions. The main floor accommodates a medical practice, the floor below it contains a small apartment in addition to utility rooms. On the second floor the doctor's own apartment is located and, above it, under the eaves, is still another apartment which has something of the character of a maisonette thanks to the inclusion of a small balcony cut into the roof.

The most important task of renovation was to improve the access to the various parts of the house. This was achieved by removing the central stairwell and constructing another on the side of the building. In order to insure adequate light into the apartment on the lower level, the garden was sunk nearly five feet, creating at the same time a sun-filled courtyard on the same level as the swimming pool. The garden facade was completely changed, with the new stairwell suspended in front of it. The street side and main facade were essentially preserved as they were.

1

2

3

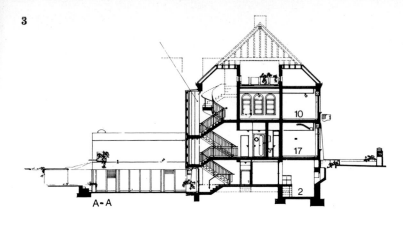

A-A

B-B

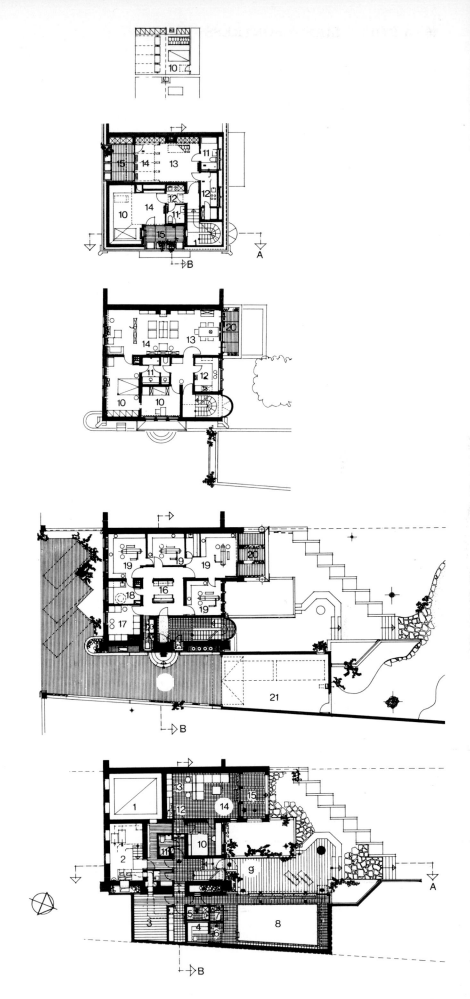

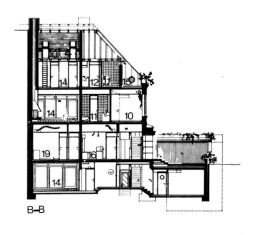

1. *View of the sunny terrace in front of the new wing with its swimming pool on the lower level.*

2. *The main facade of the building. On the right is the doorway of the garage above the pool.*

3. *Floor plans (lower level, ground floor, second and third floors) and cross section. Legend: 1 oil tank, 2 furnace, 3 storeroom, 4 sauna, 5 shower, 6 vestibule, 7 toilet, 8 pool, 9 terrace, 10 bedrooms, 11 baths, 12 kitchens, 13 dining areas, 14 living rooms, 15 loggia, 16 reception area, 17 waiting room, 18 office, 19 examining rooms, 20 balconies, 21 garage.*

4. *View down onto the terrace with the garden beyond. On the right is the new wing with swimming pool and garage.*

5. *The new glass-and-concrete structure has been formally united to the older one of brick masonry by using corresponding materials in the layout of the outside garden and terrace levels.*

4

5

6

6. *View of the examining rooms on the main floor.*

7. *The stairwell was removed from the center of the house and placed instead on the side, forming a semicircular projection to the outside.*

7

27. EIGHT CELLAR ARCADES THROWN IN

Renovation of a Townhouse in London, England
Architects: Roy Stout and Patrick Litchfield

This house is unusual for three reasons. Its corner location means that in spite of its narrow front on the main street—barely sixteen feet wide—there is enough length along the side street to accommodate two separate entrances. Uncommonly large light shafts next to the house made it possible to use the entire basement floor as a dwelling. And finally, beyond the light well, as viewed from the house, eight brick apsoidal cellar vaults open onto the basement-level strip of courtyard. These were transformed into a garden arcade, providing a delightfully unexpected vista from the lower windows.

The central bearing wall, typical of houses of this kind, was removed and replaced by steel beams resting on partitions and supporting columns. One of the two entrances, framed for structural reasons by deep pilasters extending clear to the roof, leads directly into the smaller maisonette apartment of Pat Litchfield comprising the ground floor and basement. The other serves the larger apartment of Roy Stout on the three upper stories.

The technical difficulties encountered during renovation were considerable. The structure was in pitiful condition, the roof rotted, the long side wall disturbingly bowed toward the street, and the basement dark and damp. All these have now been forgotten thanks to the perfection of execution, the new air of spaciousness achieved by selected materials and colors, and the unified design of the whole project.

1

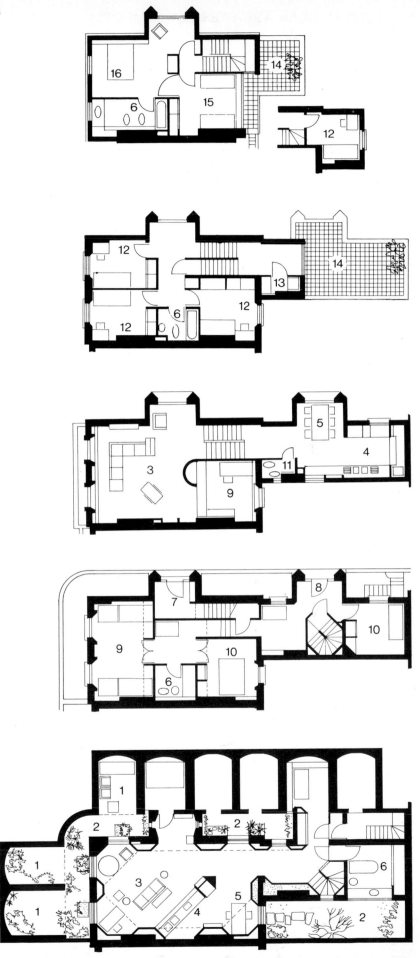

1, 2. *The building's corner site meant that in spite of its barely sixteen-foot-wide front onto the main street the length of the side wall was such that two separate entrances off the side street could easily be accommodated. One of them leads into Patrick Litchfield's smaller apartment on the ground-floor and basement levels, the other to the three upper floors comprising the larger dwelling of Roy Stout.*

3. *Floor plans (basement level, ground floor, second, third, and fourth floors, with a mezzanine between the top two stories). Legend: 1 arcades, 2 light shaft, 3 living rooms, 4 kitchens, 5 dining areas, 6 baths, 7 entry into the upper apartment, 8 entry to the lower apartment, 9 studios, 10 bedrooms, 11 toilet, 12 children's rooms, 13 utility room, 14 terraces, 15 dressing room, 16 master bedroom.*

4. The living room of the lower apartment.

5. View from one of the arcades into the living room of the lower apartment. The wide light well allows one to forget that this is the basement.

6. Seating corner in the living room of the lower apartment.

4

5

6

7. *An idyllic spot in the middle of the city. The roof terrace outside the upper apartment offers wholesome fresh air and a view, providing some of the comforts of a garden.*

8. *The living room in the upper apartment is located on the second floor. The curved wall to the left does not enclose the stairway but rather the studio.*

7

8

Renovation of a House in London, England
Architects: Spence & Webster

Aside from the construction of large studio windows on the roof, the modernization of this building was confined to the interior. But inside, the changes were so thorough that except for the floors and staircases almost nothing of the original remains. Only the round arched windows retain some of the original flavor of the interior spaces.

The transformation was particularly extensive on the ground floor. Originally this level comprised two separate rooms aside from the entry hall, one facing the street, the other facing the garden. Now there is but one large space extending from the front to the back, and the entryway and kitchen are marked off simply by a free-standing partition and a folding door near the entrance.

The design of the interior also reveals a deliberate contrast with the preserved exterior of the house. Not only was all decoration removed, but all structures, shapes, and materials were chosen for their technological overtones: the nubbly rubber floor, the track lighting, and the repeated use of rounded corners.

Structurally, the dividing wall on the ground floor was replaced by two steel beams hidden in the ceiling. These rest on the long wall opposite the kitchen on one end, and on columns integrated into the storage wall on the other.

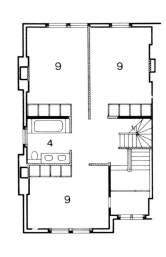

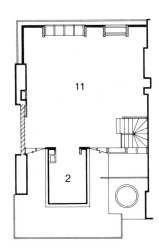

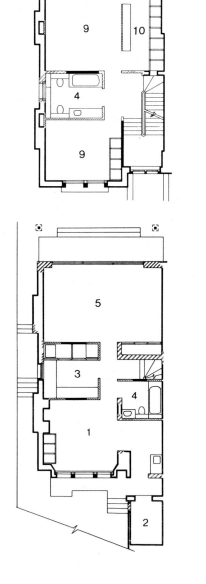

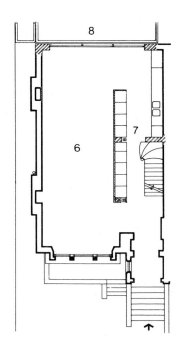

1. *Floor plans (lower level, ground floor, second, third, and fourth stories). Legend: 1 bed-sitting room, 2 storerooms, 3 utility room, 4 baths, 5 playroom, 6 living room, 7 kitchen, 8 balcony, 9 bedrooms, 10 storage, 11 studio.*

2. *Only the new studio windows on the roof betray on the outside the radical changes made to the interior of the building.*

3

3. *The living room looking toward the street. In the foreground is the dining area, and to the left, behind a room divider reaching to the ceiling, is the kitchen.*

4. *The living room looking toward the garden. The dining area is in the background.*

4

5.

5. *The studio with its wall of windows that are the sole change to the building's exterior.*

6, 7. *In order to keep the stairwell as light and airy as possible, the balustrades were reduced to simple iron frames divided horizontally by stretched wires.*

6

7

29. A GLASS SHIELD COVERS THE WHOLE FACADE

Addition to a Row House in London, England
Architects: Martin Crowley and Robin Moore-Ede

It was a typical Victorian row house, its back side unfortunately wedged into the angle between two rows of buildings so that the rear rooms were directly visible to the neighbors. Also, the view from inside was anything but inspiring, and worse, a next-door laundromat vented its dryers into the yard, befouling the whole area with their depressing, evil-smelling fumes.

A glass wall now forms an effective shield against all these nuisances, while at the same time encouraging into the structure any ray of sunlight that may stray into this maze of walls. A tubular steel framework nearly the full width of the house was stretched between the courtyard level and a point just below the existing windows three floors above. At its base, the framework is so far out from the wall that a small breakfast area could be developed; at the top, it leans against the house wall just above the level of the third-story floor; in between, it is braced on each floor by a triangulated truss, supporting planting boxes and at the second-floor level a catwalk as well. The bars supporting the wired glass extend outward from the steel framework. A system of vents at the top insures adequate circulation.

The architect writes that such a solution would no longer be permitted for a building such as this in England. According to new ordinances governing so-called preservation districts, all renovation must preserve the historical forms, regardless of functional problems or environmental nuisances—no matter how difficult continued preservation may be.

1. *Floor plans (lower level, ground floor, second and third stories). Legend: 1 bedrooms, 2 baths, 3 conservatory, 4 kitchen, 5 dining room, 6 balcony, 7 living room, 8 toilet, 9 roof garden.*

2. *The curtain of glass effectively obscures the ugliness of the surroundings. Not only did the architects wish to screen the view from without, but also to shield the house from the surroundings and create for its owners a world of their own.*

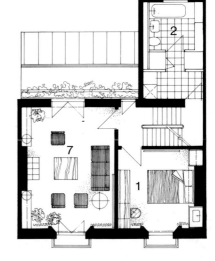

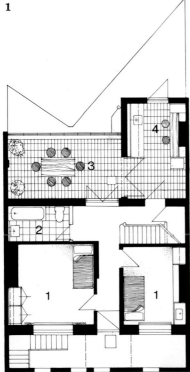

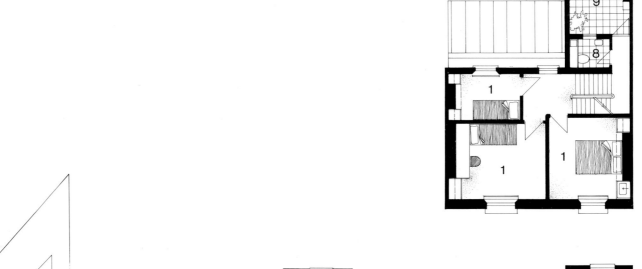

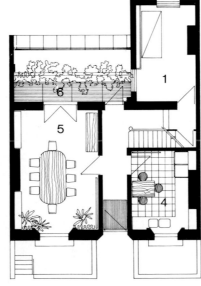

3. *A catwalk and plant boxes are supported by the triangulated trusses.*

4. *Looking upward from the courtyard one has the impression of hanging gardens.*

5. *A detailed cross section reveals the simplicity of the structure.*

6. *The glass shield has brought a new air of spaciousness to the previously cramped and narrow house.*

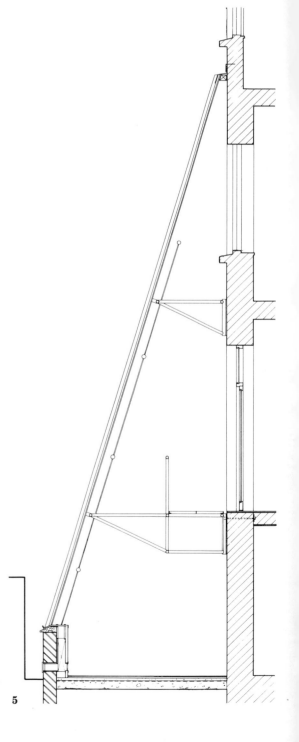

3

4 **5**

30. FROM ARTIST'S STUDIO TO DWELLING

Renovation of a Studio Building in London, England
Architect: Stephen LeRoith

These studio structures, built for successful artists around the middle of the last century, were intended to provide first-class working spaces. Very little thought was given to the possibilities of living in them. The studios were splendid, two stories high, and filled with diffuse light from the large gable windows on the north sides.

The distribution of spaces, reminiscent of row housing not so much because of the size of the rooms but because of the arrangement of walls, could be essentially preserved. The changes altered rather the function of the rooms, their access, and their illumination. As before, one first steps into a small entry hall which now, like the bedroom beyond and the living room in the former studio to the side, opens onto an enclosed courtyard with a pool and plantings. The courtyard occupies what was originally the kitchen, while the bedroom is now in the place of the small former living room. An additional bedroom is on the balcony, as in the original plan, but it has been fully enclosed. The kitchen and dining area were placed in the back part of the living area where it continues under the sleeping balcony to the back wall.

The courtyard sets the tone for the whole interior of the house most dramatically, drawing one's gaze from all corners of the rooms more than the outside windows. In addition, the surface of the pool serves splendidly to catch the light from above and reflect it into the adjacent rooms, providing them with additional illumination.

1. *View of the building from the street. On the right is the lower section with its entryway, courtyard, and smaller bedroom.*

2. *Floor plans (ground floor and second story). Legend: 1 entry, 2 toilet, 3 courtyard, 4 living room, 5 dining area, 6 kitchen, 7 baths, 8 bedrooms, 9 dressing room.*

3. *The house is one of a row of studio buildings built for successful artists in the middle of the last century.*

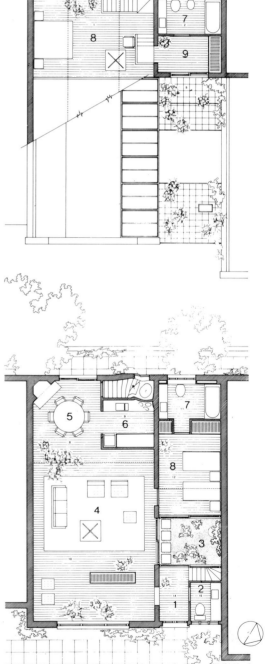

4. *View of the courtyard. In the background is the entryway, on the right the glazed portion of the mansard roof over the former studio, which now functions as a living room.*

5. *View from the smaller bedroom—here set up as a studio—of the courtyard and the entryway beyond.*

6. *The living room in the former studio looking toward the courtyard.*

7

7. *The living room looking toward the street.*

8. *Since the former kitchen was turned into the courtyard, a new kitchen had to be installed in the back part of the house.*

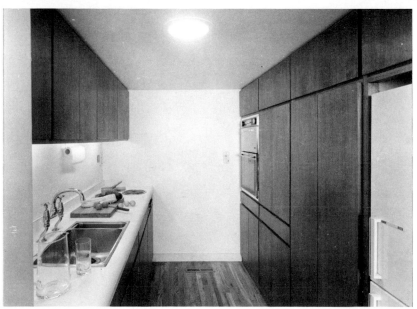

8

31. A GLASS-BRICK WALL DEFINES THE SPACE

Remodeling of an Apartment in Elkins Park, Pennsylvania, USA
Architect: Robert A. M. Stern

The apartment in a recently constructed complex had the customary sequence of small enclosed rooms, but its owner found them cold and uninviting. He therefore requested an architect to reorganize completely the floor plan, and as a result the apartment now presents a continuous series of rooms that flow into one another, the living and sleeping areas aligned along the north wall looking out at a swimming pool and the woods beyond, while the kitchen and bathrooms lie along the interior long wall.

The focus of the entire layout is an undulating wall constructed of glass bricks that allows daylight into the kitchen behind it and both delineates and expands the living area in front. At night the visual effect of the glass wall is heightened by countless tiny lights in the ceiling of the kitchen which flood the area with light, picked up also in the prisms of the wall.

In order to maximize the sense of flow from one room to the next, even the bedrooms are marked off by floor-to-ceiling sliding units that may be opened during the day.

1. *The living room looking toward the dining area. In front of the dining room a small seating area supplements the larger seating arrangement of the living room.*

2. *The living room looking toward the entry, which is behind the bookcase on the right.*

3. *Floor plan. Legend: 1 entryway, 2 toilet, 3 living room, 4 kitchen, 5 dining area, 6 bedrooms, 7 baths.*

1

2

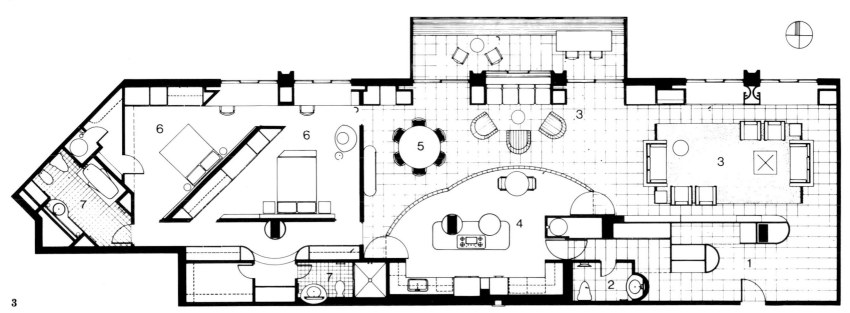

3

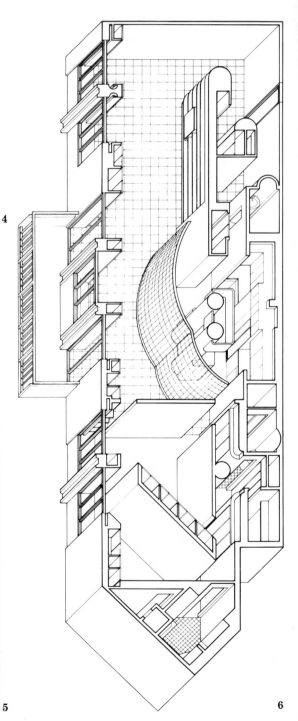

4. *The kitchen is separated from the living area by a wall of glass bricks. In the center is a cooking island, to the left a small breakfast area.*

5. *The dining area. At night the countless small lights in the ceiling of the kitchen are picked up by the individual glass units in the partition, creating a dramatic visual effect.*

6. *Axonometric floor plan.*

7. *View of the entryway. Behind the semicircle in the middle is the entrance to the kitchen and the guest toilet.*

32. AN OLD HALF-TIMBERED HOUSE REBORN

Reconstruction and Renovation of the Former Monastery Inn at Flegessen, Bad
Münder, West Germany
Architect: Klaus Pracht

The nearly 400-year-old building, its half-timbering now carefully preserved, was doomed to destruction until it was purchased by the present owner. After a full year of investigation and planning, it was decided to do away with all of its later additions. Thus partitions on all floors were removed, along with the ceilings in the main room on the ground floor and in the attic, and all plumbing and wiring. The chimneys and porches were removed, the exterior stucco taken off, and the main round-arched doorway uncovered.

The structure had to be secured by digging below the foundations, which had been destroyed by flooding and by frost, and by pouring new ones. The tiles on the roof and the west gable end had to be replaced, missing portions of the framing restored, and two new crossbeams added to the roof.

The total area of 3,500 square feet on the three floors was divided into a main dwelling, a studio, and a bachelor apartment. The studio can be converted into a third apartment if necessary, as it opens directly onto the main staircase. In case the entire house should ever serve as a single dwelling, a door was provided between the large main room of the bigger apartment and the bachelor studio.

Most striking in this example is the compromise between practical, modern use and maximum preservation of the historical structure.

1

1. *The condition of the 400-year-old house was so terrible before its renovation that it had already been destined for destruction.*

4. View through the round-arched doorway into the ground floor. In the background above the dining area is a balcony that provides access to the rooms on the second floor.

5. Floor plans (ground floor, second floor, and attic). Legend: 1 entry, 2 toilet, 3 kitchens, 4 dining areas, 5 living areas, 6 TV room, 7 studio, 8 baths, 9 bedrooms, 10 children's rooms, 11 potential kitchen area, 12 gallery.

6. A wooden spiral stair leads from the attic floor up to a loft extending like a balcony into the gallery.

7. Another view of the attic-floor gallery. The old structural elements clearly reveal the traces of traditional handicraft.

6

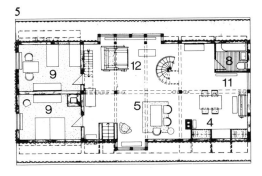

5

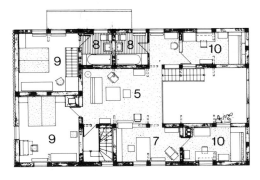

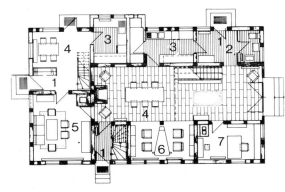

7

33. NEO-GOTHIC VS. MODERN TRANSPARENCY

Renovation and Expansion of a Park Pavilion in Hévillers, Belgium
Architect: Edouard Carlier

The former orangerie in the park of Bierbais Palace dates from the year 1828 and consisted of a long east-west wing and two taller corner pavilions with Neo-Gothic windows on the south side. The eastern half was available for conversion; it had already served as a gardener's dwelling.

Although the three floors of the pavilion offered usable space of over 2,100 square feet, the client's needs required that a one-story extension nearly 60 feet long be constructed as well. The eastern face of the new structure is slanted at 45 degrees, so that the contours of the existing pavilion are minimally affected. This diagonal portion of the end wall is reflected in a free-standing diagonal wall in front of the pavilion's east facade, providing some protection from the weather for the entry, and masking small balconies extending from the upper floors.

The pavilion itself had undergone reconstruction once before when it was converted into a house for the gardener. This time the most drastic change was the demolition of the west wall to make way for a slender metal framework supporting large panes of glass. The ground floor is divided into a two-level living room on one side, and a small office and the entry hall on the other. The second floor accommodates the master bedroom and a guest room, and the third floor has been given over to the children.

The dining room, kitchen, and two workrooms occupy the extension. The proximity of the kitchen to the living room necessitated a separate outside access.

1

2

1. *View of the house from the east. On the right is the diagonal wall of the new extension and, continuing the line of it, the free-standing wall in front of the entry into the original structure.*

2. *The garden facade seems from the distance to have been scarcely disturbed. Since the new extension is to the rear, the massive Gothic arches with their deep-set windows are the dominant architectural feature.*

3. *Floor plans (ground floor, second and third stories). Legend: 1 entry, 2 closet, 3 furnace, 4 office, 5 living room, 6 dining room, 7 kitchen, 8 sewing room, 9 laundry, 10 terrace, 11 landing, 12 master bedroom, 13 guest room, 14 baths, 15 playroom, 16 children's bedrooms.*

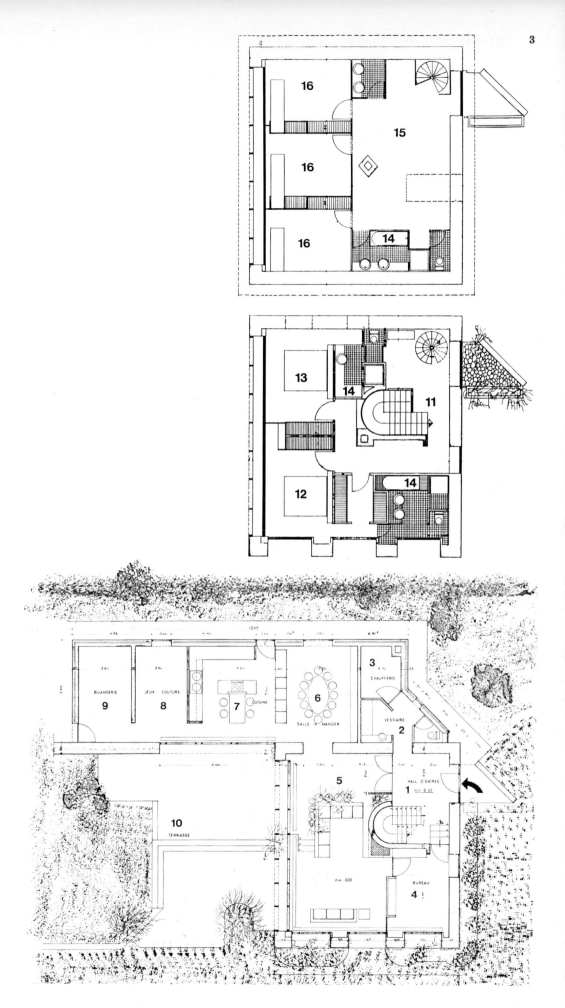

4. *View of the sunken portion of the living room.*

5

5. *The west wall of the existing building was torn down, to be replaced by a delicate structure of steel supporting a wall of glass.*

6. *View across to the old building from the kitchen in the new extension.*

6

34. MAXIMUM SPACE AT MINIMUM COST

Renovation and Expansion of a Village School in Rampton, Cambridgeshire, England
Architect: Keith Garbett

The school was a simple, two-story open structure with brick walls and a steep shingled roof, flanked on one side by a vestibule and on the other by a vaulted storeroom that once may have served as the local jail. The one-time jail became the main entryway, and the older vestibule was converted into a pantry.

While the three visible sides of the vintage 1845 schoolhouse were hardly altered, the back side of the building was radically changed by the addition of a one-story extension containing a conservatory, two bedrooms, a bath, a studio, and the garage. The schoolroom itself was given a two-level balcony. On the main floor are the entry, the living area, dining area, and kitchen, while on the lower of the two balcony levels are a bathroom and dressing area, and on the upper one the master bedroom.

The whole project was accomplished for very little money, largely because the owner, an industrial designer and accomplished carpenter, shared in the planning and did much of the inside finish work himself.

1. *The three sides of the vintage 1845 building visible from the street were little changed. In the left foreground is a one-story addition that may have been the local jail at one time.*

1

2. *View from the garden of the old building and the staggered walls of the extension.*

3. *Old and new are kept clearly distinct, both in form and in use of materials. The addition is obviously modern.*

143

4. *View from the living room in the original structure toward the conservatory in the extension. In the background is the small courtyard.*

5. *The owner, an industrial designer, maintains a studio in the extension.*

4

5

144

6. *Floor plans (ground floor, upper levels).*
Legend: 1 entry yard, 2 garage, 3 entry,
4 living room, 5 kitchen, 6 dining area, 7 pantry,
8 conservatory, 9 baths, 10 courtyard,
11 bedrooms, 12 studio, 13 tool room, 14 dressing
room, 15 master bedroom.

7. *The living room is open up to the eaves. In*
the background is the two-level balcony with
the parents' sleeping area, below which are
located the kitchen and dining area.

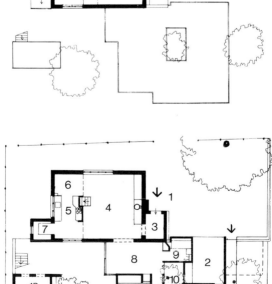

6

7

35. A COLORFUL MIX OF NEW USES

Renovation of Two Warehouses in Copenhagen, Denmark
Architects: Dissing + Weitling

The two seventeenth-century warehouses stand proudly next to the Christianhavn Canal, on a former freight-loading wharf. Though they are protected as landmarks, a total renovation of the interiors was permissible, as well as minor alteration of the facades. From the second floor upward the two structures were connected on each level by up to three doors broken through the connecting firewall so that the whole interior complex is served by a single stairwell.

Work began in the top floors, as these were the first to fall vacant. The architects moved their offices into the two attic levels. The ground floor accommodated a restaurant on one side and parking space for six cars on the other. The three remaining stories were converted into condominiums, each occupying an entire level of a building. The placement of the window openings in the facades permitted a perfectly reasonable arrangement of rooms. The old partitions were completely removed and each level totally redesigned. The bearing posts, beams, and rafters were left exposed, and new walls were arranged quite independently of them.

The original facades were scarcely changed, with their typical shutters preserved wherever possible. The openings were fitted with mullioned windows in imitation of those characteristic of older buildings in the vicinity.

1. *The east front before renovation.*

2. *The east front after renovation was complete.*

3. *The converted warehouses offer a commanding view of the canal. A ship's mast obscures the dividing line between the two structures, causing them to appear as a single unit.*

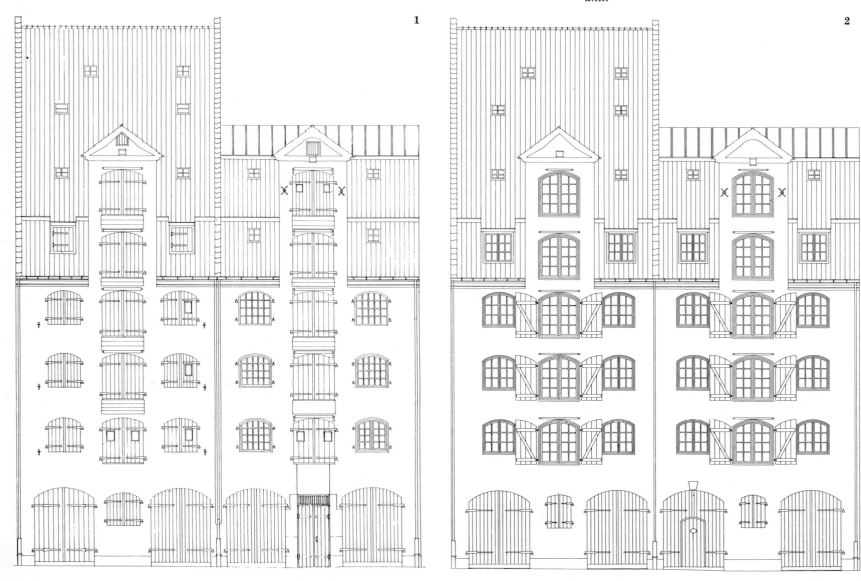

1

2

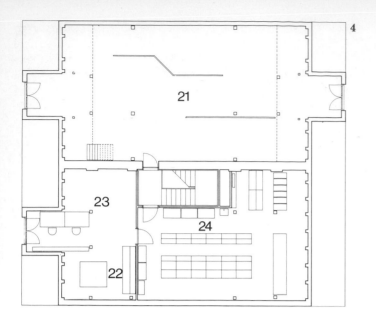

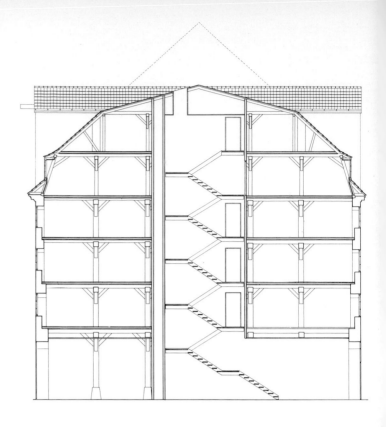

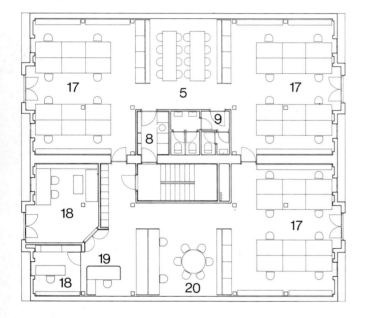

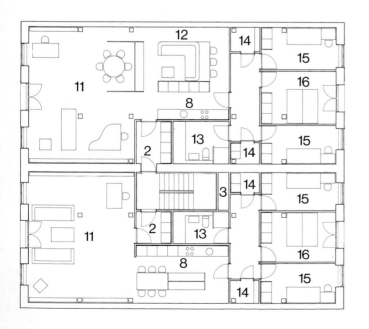

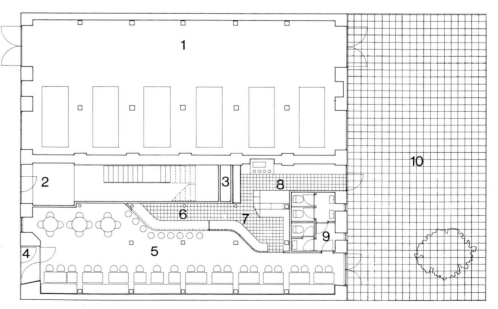

4. *Floor plans (ground floor, a representative middle floor, and lower and upper attic floors) and cross section. Legend: 1 garage, 2 entry, 3 air shaft, 4 restaurant entrance, 5 dining rooms, 6 bar, 7 buffet, 8 kitchens, 9 toilets, 10 terrace, 11 living rooms, 12 seating area, 13 baths, 14 storerooms, 15 children's rooms, 16 master bedrooms, 17 drafting rooms, 18 offices, 19 reception, 20 consulting room, 21 exhibition space, 22 model-making, 23 photography, 24 archives.*

5. *The existing partitions were completely removed and each floor totally reorganized. The contrast between the massive old structural elements and the sleek, modern built-ins is particularly striking.*

6. *View of one of the living rooms.*

5

6

149

7. *The larger of the two office rooms in the architects' studio. In the background on the left is the reception area.*

8. *Consultation area and one of the three drafting rooms in the architects' studio.*

7

8

9. *A drafting room in the architects' studio.*

10. *The architects' dining room. Track-light spots and hanging lamps suspended from conduits running below the beams reveal the architects' desire to keep old and new elements distinct and separate, especially structural elements and modern additions.*

10

36. BOXES FOR INTIMACY

Renovation of a Loft Building Floor in New York City, USA
Architect: Jon Michael Schwarting

The assignment was to preserve the characteristic structure of the large loft, yet attempt to create the intimate spaces expected in an apartment. The architect achieved both by placing big boxlike structures in the larger space, dividing it adequately without destroying its old features.

A studio was set up on the deck of the larger box, a bedroom above the smaller one. Inside the larger are two smaller bedrooms, and the smaller box contains the kitchen. The remaining open space is shared by the living and dining areas.

The boxes are set back from the walls and well below the ceilings so that one easily recognizes them to be new intrusions into the space. The design capitalizes on contrast. While the larger space with its Corinthian columns, its fussily ornamental ceiling, and its large pilastered windows has a pleasantly over-decorated feeling, the large unbroken surfaces of the new partitions, cleanly cut here and there by functional openings, project a monumental calm. In order to make the confrontation as gentle as possible, however, everything but the floors, the staircases, and the banisters was painted a unifying white.

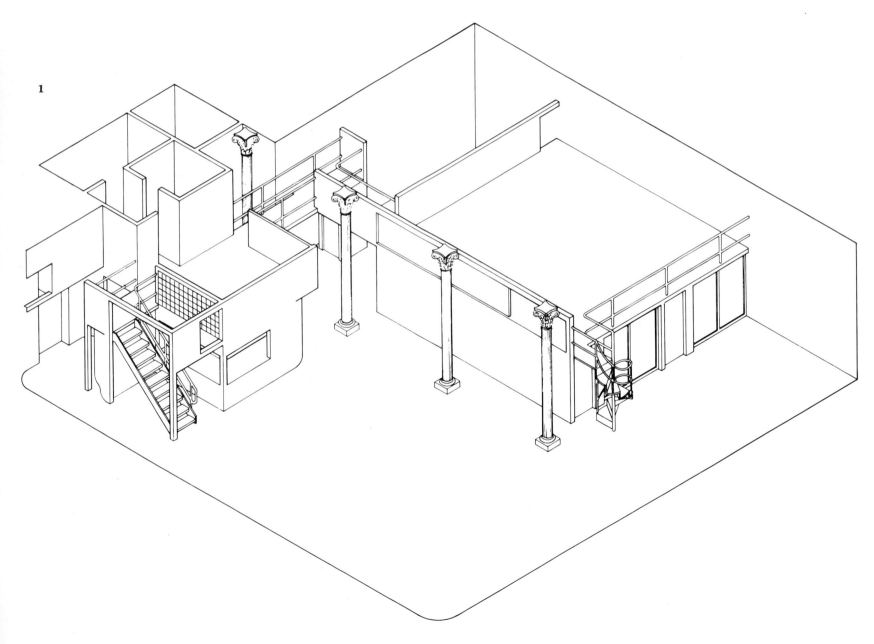

1

1. *Axonometric floor plan.*

2. *Floor plans (lower and upper levels).*
Legend: 1 kitchen, 2 utility room, 3 bath,
4 living area, 5 dining area, 6 bedrooms,
7 studio.

3, 4. *It was hoped that the characteristic*
feeling of the larger loft area could be
preserved while at the same time creating the
smaller, intimate spaces one expects of living
areas. The two large boxes that the architect
placed into the room provide a solution,
structuring the space without compromising it.

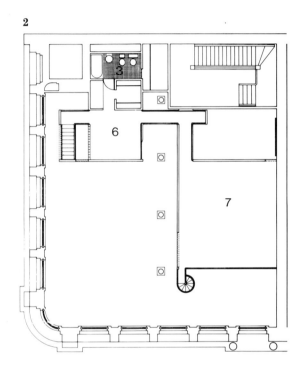

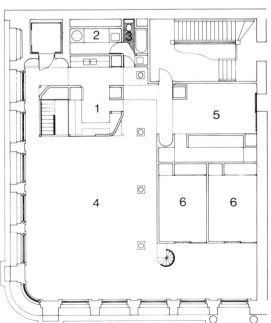

153

5. *The Corinthian columns, the ornamental
tin ceiling, and the pilastered window openings
give the larger space a charmingly fussy
feeling. The new partitions, by contrast, with
their gleaming white smooth surfaces, seem
soothingly austere and calm.*

6. *The new structures leave a considerable amount of space open to the ceiling; in this way they seem like pieces of furniture rather than whole room constructions. Here the sleeping loft above the kitchen.*

7. *The dining area between the stairwell (left) and the new unit with two bedrooms inside and a studio above (right). The large sliding door in the background serves only to cover the dish cupboard.*

6

7

37. COTTON BALES WERE ONCE STORED HERE

Conversion of a Warehouse in Savannah, Georgia, USA
Architect: Juan C. Bertotto

This building on the banks of the Savannah River, with its solid masonry walls of fieldstone and brick, is certified to be the oldest cotton warehouse on the east coast of America. It was built in 1816, and it is one of the most notable architectural monuments from the early days of the city. The building is framed on the east and west by newer structures; the two remaining sides have access to streets, though the street entrance on the south lies three floors below the corresponding access on the north.

The two lower floors now contain shops, while the fourth and fifth floors have been converted into the new owner's own dwelling. The unfinished third floor may one day become a part of this apartment.

The exterior of the building was left untouched. Only a staircase up to the second-floor shop was added on the north, and on the south two entrance bridges.

In the design of the interior the architect was determined to link the various living areas as closely together as possible: on the fourth floor, the living room, library, dining area, and kitchen are indicated rather than separated by curved partitions that stop short of the ceiling. A large cut through the ceiling provides a visual tie to the floor above. The huge wooden wheel suspended above this opening once served to raise and lower the bales of cotton five floors above the wharf.

1. Floor plans (fourth and fifth floors) and cross section. Legend: 1 entry, 2 kitchen, 3 dining area, 4 living room, 5 library, 6 baths, 7 master bedroom, 8 daughter's room, 9 balcony, 10 son's room, 11 laundry, 12 equipment and storage.

2. Street facade of the building on the south side. The bridges across to the two upper floors are new.

3. The north side facing the river. The staircase leading up to the second-story tea shop is all that has been added.

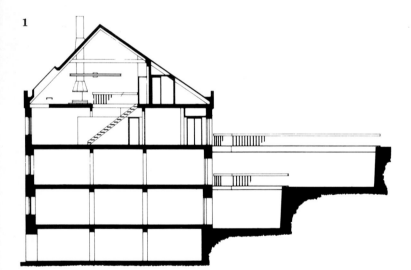

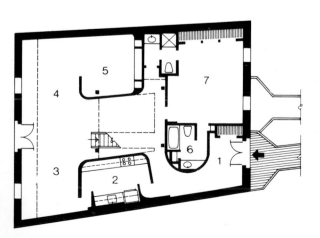

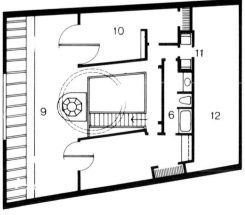

4.

4. *View from the balcony into the son's room. The wide revolving door is most unusual.*

5. *The fourth-floor living room looking toward the dining area. On the left beyond the stairs is the kitchen, set off distinctly from the older structural elements.*

6. *View across the opening cut between the fourth and fifth floors. Below is the living room; on the balcony above is an open fireplace.*

5

INDEX OF NAMES

PHOTO CREDITS